The
15-Minute
Clean

Published in 2021 by Welbeck,
An imprint of Welbeck Non-Fiction Limited,
Part of of the Welbeck Publishing Group

20 Mortimer Street
London W1T 3JW

A CIP catalogue for this book is available from the British Library.

ISBN 978-1-78739-613-5

Printed in Dubai

10 9 8 7 6 5 4 3 2 1

LYNSEY CROMBIE
TV's QUEEN OF CLEAN

The
15-Minute
Clean

The quickest way
to a sparkling home

WELBECK

Contents

Introduction

Do you feel like your home always looks as if a bomb has gone off? Trust me, I get it! When my children were younger, and I was at home looking after them, my house was such a mess. Sometimes, I used to really struggle just to get out of the door because I was always cleaning and tidying. There never seemed to be enough hours in the day to get my house in order. What I didn't realize then is that with an efficient plan of 5-, 10- and 15-minute tasks that you complete every day, having a spotless house isn't just achievable – it's easy.

When it's your day off and numerous low-key activities are calling you, such as meeting a friend for a dog walk, that yoga class you are desperate to try out or a novel your friend recommended, the last thing you want is to be stuck at home cleaning.

The problem is you have already set yourself up for failure by saving all of your cleaning and housework for just one day and without any sort of plan.

Having a clean and tidy house may not be the answer to all of life's problems, but after a hectic week at work, it certainly helps. Doing little tasks throughout the week – before and after work for example, and involving the rest of the family – will give you more time to spend with family and friends at the weekends.

We all know that once you start cleaning, it could go on for hours or even all day if you really let time run away from you. Training yourself to do short but intensive bursts of cleaning for 5, 10 or 15 minutes every day can help you achieve a clean and organized home. All you need to do is set a timer and when it goes off, you stop! With a total of 15 minutes cleaning every day, you can have a beautifully clean and tidy home. It's as simple as that. Use your phone, your cooker clock or a stopwatch, and let the time restriction motivate you.

In this book, I have put together simple plans to help keep you motivated and help to you to stay top of your housework – this means you'll have more time for yourself and your loved ones. When you run a busy household, the key to keeping it manageable is creating and maintaining a daily routine. This is not just about housework. You need to factor in sleep, self-care, childcare, healthy diet and exercise – there's always so much to do. After reading this book, you'll be able to plan your daily 15-minute Clean, and a personalized 30-day Plan, which will completely change how you approach cleaning – giving you back valuable time to do what you love and look after yourself, as well as your friends and family.

When life gets hectic, self-care practically flies out of the window – but if you want to successfully maintain everything, then it is going to become your new best friend. You need to feel energetic, refreshed and motivated to tackle the challenges life throws at you. Self-care Sunday puts me on track for the week ahead, so when I wake up on Monday I am ready to write my weekly to-do list and face what lies ahead.

This book really will change the way you tackle your household tasks, meaning you really can set aside a time every week just for you – and still have a spotless home.

Easy, Every Day

There are some areas in the home that I believe need attention every single day. By doing these tasks daily you will stay on top of everyday messes — and they will only take up a few seconds of your time. You should consider these basic tasks to be daily habits that you do without even thinking, and not necessarily as part of cleaning plans and schedules, as you need a good base upon which to build your new 15-minute cleaning routine. There are also some simple changes you can make to save you time and hassle, like sourcing the right equipment and getting your to-do lists organized.

Have the right cleaning tools

The first thing you need to address is having the right toolkit for your daily cleaning habits that should get done as a matter of course, and will take no time at all. I really can't emphasize enough just how important it is to have the correct tools for your home when completing your daily cleaning habits.

There are, of course, several ways to organize your cleaning kit, and it really boils down to your storage situation and preferences. You could have everything stored in one central spot (i.e. a cleaning cupboard), but if you have the space, the best solution is to divide up your kit and leave it in various points around your home, while keeping large and infrequently used items in your main cleaning storage point. Storing specific tools nearest to where you need them keeps cleaning time to a minimum, and ensures you don't waste time looking for cleaning products. To make your daily cleaning habits easier, keep a small supply of basics in relevant areas of your home – for example, a bottle of bleach, a general disinfectant and a stack of cloths in your bathroom – in a tidy caddy.

You could also choose to store and carry items in your mop bucket or plastic tubs. Buckets are really useful for obvious cleaning tasks, but I like them because they are also great for soaking cleaning cloths in disinfectant after use, and convenient for transporting items around the home.

Tools I recommend

Cordless vacuum
These are perfect for quick cleaning with no fuss and no time spent attending to cords.

Flat-headed microfibre mop
I find these much better for actually picking up dirt rather than pushing it around as regular mops do.

Steamer
Not one that just does the floors, but one that has extra tools that can tackle other jobs in your home. Steam kills germs without the need for chemicals, so is especially helpful for anyone with allergies. Use your steamer for floors, hard surfaces, toilet, glass, refreshing upholstery and removing creases from clothes.

Colour-coded microfibre cloths
The colour coding helps keep order within your cleaning system – you don't want to be cleaning your sink with the cloth that has just scrubbed your toilet. Create your own coded system or follow mine:

• Blue for loo

• Pink for sink

• Green for glass

• Yellow for mellow (light dusting)

• Silver/grey for stainless steel

Rags
When bath towels have come to the end of their lives, repurpose them by cutting them up. As cleaning rags, they are exactly the right texture for picking up dirt and helpful for any outside cleaning.

Sponges

Dusting glove
These are great for quickly tackling slatted blinds and other surfaces that frequently collect dust.

Toothbrush
If their bristles are in decent nick, disinfect your old ones and use them to access hard-to-reach areas.

Long-handled duster

Squeegee
Store one in the shower to wipe down surfaces after use, helping to stop the accumulation of water marks and limescale.

Dustpan and brush
This one's a classic pairing that never goes out of fashion, precisely because it's always handy for little accidents, and the brush is ideal for tackling window tracks.

Stair brush
Refresh your stair carpets in a pinch and when you don't want to get the vacuum out.

Bucket

Everyday disinfecting

If you have extra time, don't waste it: disinfect your high-traffic door handles, TV remote controls, light switches and mobile phone.

When you are out and about, your mobile phone is often placed on coffee-shop tables, the floor, contactless payment points, your car, your desk and countless other places, or else it's left to float around your handbag. Numerous studies have found that your phone harbours far more germs than the average toilet seat.

Spray product on to a cloth, remove your phone case and gently wipe the device over. Pop the case in a warm bowl of water and then dry it off before putting it back on. Another great way to clean your mobile phone, and even your car keys, is to pop them into a UV light box for 30 seconds. While the machine is working, don't waste those 30 seconds – find something quick and constructive to do. See overleaf for how to clean your phone properly. After you've done your disinfecting, make sure you wash your hands too – see pages 20–21 for how to clean hands properly.

Daily Cleaning Habits Checklist

Each of the tasks listed below should be super quick.

- [ ] Clean up messes as they happen, like carpet stains or marks from sticky fingers

- [ ] Encourage household members to pick up after themselves

- [ ] Air out your home, throw open those windows and let the fresh air in. Fresh air is great for eliminating odours and will make your home feel refreshed

- [ ] Wash up or pop dishes in the dishwasher after every meal (encourage others in the house to get into this habit, too)

- [ ] Use as little equipment as possible when cooking to save yourself tidying up time – there are some great one-pot recipe ideas out there that will save you washing up

- [ ] Sweep a vacuum over the kitchen floor, high-traffic areas and home entrances – using a cordless vacuum saves you the time it takes to plug it in, wrangle the cord around furniture, unplug it, and wind up the cord

- [ ] Wipe down the kitchen table after eating and put away table mats

- [ ] Wipe down kitchen surfaces, especially the areas where food has been prepared

- [ ] After a bath or shower, wipe wet surfaces using a microfibre cloth (or keep a squeegee to hand) to stop the build-up of water marks and limescale

- [ ] Wipe down the toilet seat with bleach or use a denture tablet

- [ ] When needed, wash, fold and put away a load of laundry, alternating between dark and light loads.

How To Clean Your Hands

1. Put hand sanitizer or soap and warm water onto your hands

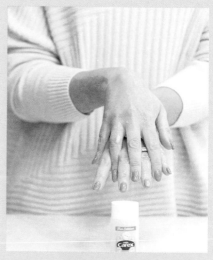

2. Rub your palms together

3. Clean the backs of your hands and in between your fingers by placing one hand on top of another and rubbing – repeat with the second hand

4. Interlace your fingers palm to palm and rub your hands together

5. Clean the backs of your fingers by rubbing them against your palms

6. Rub each thumb

7. Clean the palms of each hand with the tips of your fingers from your other hand

What next?

Now we have established what our daily habits should include, but what about the rest of the housework? Modern life places a lot of demands on our time, and running a home is challenging, especially if you're often busy or live with multiple people. I have always found that "little and often" works best, in conjunction with having a solid structure in place.

Your 15-minute Clean and accompanying 30-day Plan, alongside your family schedule and daily to-do lists, are essential – sure to bring you satisfaction every time you tick something off.

My Household Cleaning Tasks List includes most jobs a home will need doing on a monthly basis. It's a pretty big list, and no one would want to do them all in one day! It's all about breaking these tasks up into manageable chunks and involving other household members if you can. Who on earth wants to spend their spare time cleaning? I certainly don't, and by following my simple schedules, I never have to.

Household cleaning tasks

To get into good order, we need to start by writing a list of all the household tasks your home needs. Use the examples on page 24 as a base for completing your own list of household cleaning tasks – walk from room to room, and meticulously around every room, making a note of every task required. This way you won't miss anything, and you'll be able to build really thorough 15-minute Cleans and a 30-day Plan.

Tip: Put it away, not down

The simplest of tasks that will save you so much time! One of the best new habits you can build is putting things where they belong straight away. So much mess can be averted entirely by tidying items away and not just dumping them anywhere.

Household Cleaning Tasks List

* Cleaning internal windows

* Cleaning mirrors

* Vacuuming

* Mopping or steaming hard floors

* Cleaning skirting boards

* Cleaning internal doors

* Cleaning the fridge

* Tackling clutter hotspots

* Organizing paperwork

* Sorting kids' or pets' toys

* Cleaning under beds

* Washing net curtains and curtains

* Polishing windowsills

* Deep cleaning kitchen appliances

* Cleaning inside and outside of kitchen cabinets

* Disinfecting door handles

* Deep cleaning the shower and shower head

* Cleaning bathroom sink and plug holes

Once completed, this list can seem endless, but all these jobs need to be done to keep our homes in order.

Household Cleaning Tasks List

Household Cleaning Tasks List

Household Cleaning Tasks List

Split your home up

Split your home into rooms, so you can create a plan per room.
A good way to do this is to think of your home as a square.
Then, divide it up into quarters and do a quarter at a time.

Break your bad cleaning habits

Naturally, we are constantly on the lookout for ways to make our cleaning tasks faster and easier. However, making these shortcuts is not always the right thing to do and sometimes it even makes the job harder and more time-consuming.

Bad cleaning habits can actually cause harm to your home. By breaking these habits now and getting out of your own way, you can work faster and more efficiently in the long run.

The 13 worst cleaning habits

1) Too much product
Using too much cleaning product is one of the worst mistakes to make. If we're all being honest, I think we can hold our hands up and say that we have been there ... and used practically half a bottle of product to clean one small area. Skincare advisors always tell us that a little goes a long way, and this rule is exactly the same in the cleaning industry.

Leftover cleaning residue that hasn't quite been rinsed off becomes a magnet for trapping dirt and dust, while using too much laundry detergent can clog up your washing machine, causing long-term complications and expense.

Cleaning products have instruction labels for a reason – read them and adhere to the stated quantities.

2) Forgetting to clean the things that clean for you
The things that clean for you, such as your dishwasher, washing machine, floor mop, vacuum and cloths, all need to be kept cared for to help you do a good job.

It is easy to overlook these items, but how can you expect a clean house if your tools are filthy?

Too busy to clean out your vacuum, so instead you just leave it until the dust is shooting out the back, leaving a path of debris and dust? If you try to use it when it's full like this, it will lose much of its suction and you will notice that your carpet lines disappear – or the roller could be stiff and unusable from a collection of hair and dust that was never cleaned out. By cleaning your vacuum regularly, it will run much better and speed up your cleaning.

If you have a corded vacuum, make sure it is unplugged before you start to clean it. Empty out the dust compartment and clean using warm soapy water, rinsing well. Put soap and warm water on a cloth to wipe down the exterior, and remove the hair from the roller.

If your washing machine has a nasty odour, then let's be honest: your clothes are going to stink. No matter how much detergent you use, the stale smell won't go away.

Take some time to thoroughly clean your cleaning tools, and add them into your plans and schedules.

3) Wearing shoes in the house
Always remove your shoes in your home entrances and never be tempted to run upstairs and grab something you have forgotten with your shoes on. By not wearing shoes at all in your home, you save a lot of time vacuuming.

Make this habit second nature for everyone in your home by providing a shoe zone or basket in your entrance area.

4) Not making your bed every day
An unmade bed can make the rest of the room, even if it is clean and tidy, look messy. Making your bed only takes up a small amount of your time, but has a big impact on the look of the room and the mindset of the occupant. If you have children, this is a habit you should encourage from a young age, as it helps keep the rest of the space neat as well.

When selecting bedding, go for simple, less fussy options – in the long run, you will be glad you did. Another way to keep bed-making low effort and high reward? Don't have too many scatter cushions; putting these back on becomes an extra job in itself.

5) Letting the cleaning build up

I am a big fan of the idea of "little and often", hence why I developed my 5-minute Challenge. When you do absolutely no cleaning or tidying all week and leave it until it becomes overwhelming, you put unnecessary strain on yourself and your mental health. Remember that a tidy house = a tidy mind.

6) Cleaning your windows on sunny days

When the sun is shining, we definitely feel more motivated to grab that squeegee, rush outside and clean the windows. But this is a huge mistake.

As soon as you apply product, the sun will dry it, and this will cause streaks. In sunny weather, choose to clean your windows in the late afternoon or evening or wait until you get an overcast sky.

7) Not allowing product to work

When using product on high-traffic and tough-to-clean areas, allow the product to actually work. Just spraying and wiping isn't always enough, and is not guaranteed to kill germs and bacteria.

Spray your product and allow it to sit for at least a minute before you rinse away. While the product is sitting, use this time to tackle another cleaning job in the same vicinity.

8) Using too much water on your hard floors

Oversaturation is, unsurprisingly, not good for your hard floors, and can cause damage by soaking into scratches and gaps. When shopping for floor-cleaning products, choose one that is formulated specifically for your floor type, and always follow the instructions.

9) Using hot water for everything

Not everyone knows this, but cold water can be better for cleaning stains. Hot water will set some stains, in particular protein-based ones such as blood, dairy, baby food, mud and sweat.

So, opt for a cold-water flush of the affected area under the tap as soon as you can. Do this with the garment inside out, as this forces the stain to the surface and makes it easier to remove.

10) Vacuuming with no strategy

If you use the correct vacuuming technique, you can speed up your cleaning. Always work from the top of the room to the bottom. Begin vacuuming with the brush head and remove any cobwebs from the ceiling. Then clean the tops of things, such as your wardrobes, picture frames, picture rails, light fittings, window frames, windowsills and skirting boards.

When you have finished with the brush head, switch to the main head and start off by cleaning underneath furniture before you do the main part of the room.

Once you finish vacuuming, you can refresh your carpets using a fabric refresher.

Fabric Refresher Recipe

Try making your own using a spray bottle, water, bicarbonate of soda and your favourite essential oil.

Add two tablespoons of bicarbonate of soda to the bottle (using a funnel streamlines this and keeps it tidy), and add in 20 drops of your chosen essential oil. Fill with water and shake well.

11) Choosing rough materials to clean stainless steel
When cleaning stainless steel, many of us will go for more abrasive cleaning cloths and sponges, as this is what the shops sell and market to us. But many of these may permanently scratch our stainless-steel appliances. To keep your stainless-steel appliances unsullied, choose a clean, soft cloth and use hot water.

12) Not understanding your surfaces
When choosing a cleaning product, it is crucial to know your surface. For instance, is your wooden table bare timber, or does it have an acrylic finish? If you do not know, try to find out. The same rule applies to any surface you are working on – all surfaces react in different ways to cleaning products and cleaning utensils.

13) Not making it easier for yourself

One of the most hated cleaning jobs is vacuuming the stairs. No one really likes dragging a heavy vacuum up and down, but you can help yourself and make this task much more bearable. You may have an ornate staircase or a plain and functional one, but no matter what type it is, they do need to be vacuumed every week. Stairs are a dust haven.

Start vacuuming from the top of the stairs and work your way down, because dust lifts and drops. As you go over each step, vacuum in-between the bannister posts using the nozzle or brush attachment. Then vacuum by facing the stairs, and always keep the machine in front of you for your safety.

If your stairs are wooden, the speediest method is to vacuum and then wipe with a mop. Dust any picture frames you may have along the stairwell with a damp cloth, and dust and polish bannisters according to their material.

A quick tip: Before vacuuming, run up and down the stairs a few times to dislodge as much of the dust as possible. This has the additional benefit of also being great exercise for you or a fun task to delegate to the kids.

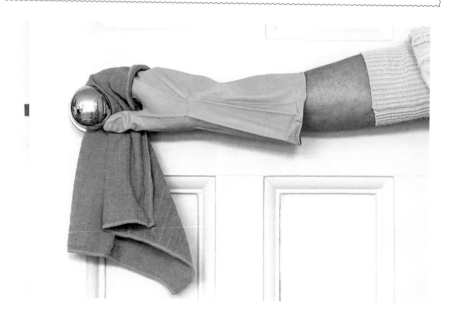

Where to start when cleaning a room

Sometimes knowing where to start when cleaning a room can feel overwhelming. Remember that one of the most efficient ways to get it done is to work from the top to the bottom, always keeping in mind that dust falls.

Starting at the top is a favourite with professional cleaners, who choose to work this way so that they never have to clean anything twice.

When you clean a room in this manner, you are working with gravity rather than against it. Look around your room, scan the tallest areas and start there. Allow the dust and dirt you've brought down to fall to the floor. Never clean the floors until you have finished tackling everything in the room, or you'll be making more work for yourself.

Follow this simple step-by-step process:

Step 1: Dusting
Start with the tallest areas in your room. Grab your long-handled duster and reach up high to tackle any cobwebs that could be around your light fittings and on your ceilings. This may require a stepstool or ladder, if you have one, or else a sturdy chair.

Then move on to the tallest surfaces such as wardrobes, bookcases and other tall units. I find that flat-headed dusters are ideal for these areas.

Continue this, moving lower and lower until you have done all of your surfaces.

Step 2: Time to clean
Now that the dust is out of the way, it is time to actually wipe or disinfect the surfaces. Grab a damp duster and your favourite all-purpose cleaning product, again working from top to bottom.

Step 3: Floor time
Now that you've completed the rest of the cleaning, you are free to clean the floors, using your vacuum to suck up the fallen dust and dirt.

If you do feel your vacuum pulling and struggling, it's time to clean it out and wash the filter.

Step 4: Stand back
Just like that, you are done. Stand back and feel proud of your tidy, clean room.

Tip: You may worry that by saving the vacuuming until the end you are allowing a quicker dust to build up in your vacuum. This may have been the case years ago, but modern vacuums have highly efficient filters that help keep the dirt trapped inside.

Try the follow-the-wall cleaning technique

The follow-the-wall cleaning technique is exactly what it sounds like – it's all about following the wall a bit like you do a road map. You start in one corner of the room and work your way around by following the wall, helping to ensure that you don't miss anything that needs your attention.

Eventually, you complete a full circuit of your home, including those often-overlooked spots that you tend to put off for as long as possible (for example, that dead space behind your sofa, which serves as a great hiding space for items with no real home). This technique sees to it that every part of your room is looked at in a streamlined and systematic way.

I learnt about this rule when I was a domestic cleaner. A lady I cleaned for had once employed a full-time housekeeper in her rather large family home and this was the method her housekeeper had adopted so that she never missed a thing. I have since discovered that many professional cleaners use this technique.

The follow-the-wall technique is a great orderly approach to your household cleaning that can really help simplify your routine and keep you on top of your housework.

My top tip with this method is to finish in your "worst" room, as this is normally the most labour intensive.

Three reasons why you should try the follow-the-wall technique

– You will feel more motivated

A great benefit of this strategy is that it produces more obvious results. This addresses one of the major drawbacks of cleaning by task (instead of by area), which is that it can leave you feeling as though you have little to show for your efforts.

But when you clean by following the wall, each area will look pristine when you're finished. When you're able to clearly see the results of your efforts, you'll feel more motivated to keep going. Keep your cleaning caddy with you as you follow the wall, stocked with every product you're going to need in that room.

– Do it your way

You can adapt the follow-the-wall technique to fit into any cleaning schedule. Following the walls in your home will give you a clear beginning and end point to work from. Try this technique when you do the 5-minute Challenge, and I bet in the long run it will save you even more time.

– You will be much more thorough

When you follow the wall, it makes it harder to skip past or forget certain tasks. Those easy- to-forget areas tend to be under the bed, in the hallway cupboard and behind your sofa. This way, if you're working on a section of wall with a window, it'll be much easier to remember to dust the blinds before you move on!

How to create a functional workspace at home

Many of us are now taking full advantage of modern technologies and setting up workstations to do our jobs, part-time or full-time, from home.

I have worked from home for years; in the early days, I was just perched at the edge of my dining-room table, but I was never fully productive. I was distracted by everything, from the postperson knocking to a fun feature on morning TV. If your home is untidy or dirty, this will also distract you from your work, so it's really important you keep everything neat and clean so you can focus on the tasks at hand.

With the way the world has changed due to both advancements in technology and the coronavirus pandemic, we need to make sure we are productive working from home and can create a quiet space with few distractions. It is easier said than done, especially if you live in a busy or compact household, but I hope that these tips can help you create the perfect oasis to get through your work to-do lists.

Home office

If you are lucky enough to have a home that already has a home office, then this bit is obvious – that is the perfect place for you to hide yourself away and focus. If not, try and find somewhere where you can actually shut the door. If you are deciding between a shared common area or a bedroom, choose a bedroom. Generally, these rooms are less busy during the day and you get the option to shut the door. The last thing you want is to be disrupted by people coming home from work and school and making cups of tea or putting on the TV.

If a bedroom isn't a good option for you, it's time to get creative. Your home may possess a cleverly designed nook, cranny or recess that could certainly do the trick, or you may have an unused corner somewhere – in the hallway, under the stairs, in a messy walk-in wardrobe or an awkward dead space in which you have parked a large vase or unused bookcase. All of these are candidates for a transformation into a handy work area.

Lighting

Make sure you set your space up somewhere in your home with good lighting. Your table or desk, or whatever your work surface is, should be placed near a window if possible, so you get some natural light. Whether you have a window or not, you will want to bring in some extra lighting. When you are working, you don't want to be straining to see what you are doing, and if you are doing meetings over Skype or Zoom with work colleagues you need to make sure they can actually see you well.

Power

Make sure your workspace is either located next to a power outlet or can be reached by an extension cord. If you are going to be doing a lot of video calls, test this out to make sure you are happy with the background, lighting, sound and the quality of the call. Test the Wi-Fi signal – you don't want it dropping out in the middle of an important call. You may find that some areas in your home have a better Wi-Fi connection then others, or that certain times of the day (when other people's devices may be off the home network) are better for calls or downloads,

Seating

Being comfortable and looking after your posture is vital when working from home. If you have your own office, then get a good sturdy office chair. If you have set yourself up in a room, try to match up a chair or table that works with that room. A cushion or a blanket can help make your seat a bit more comfortable, but you should have proper back support – hunching over a computer is not going to do you any good.

Another great option is to consider devising a standing desk, using a surface such as your kitchen worktop. You may need to grab a couple of books to pop under your laptop to get the right height, but standing desks are now quite popular because they help to keep your body moving. Whether you have chosen to sit or stand, create a setup that keeps your back aligned and stops you bending down to see the screen. You can also incorporate quick stretching routines into your day, to make sure your body doesn't become stiff and achy from staying in one position too long – there are loads of videos and routines available online.

Do not work from your bed or sofa. It may seem cosy, but working in your bed is a big mistake. If you associate your bed with work, you will have trouble falling asleep at night.

Similarly, sitting in the same spot on your sofa to work as you do for your Netflix binge will feel so much less relaxing when you try to switch off at the end of a hard day.

Even in a small home, try your best to create a workspace that is separate from your relaxation zone.

Create a filing system

If you do have an office, then use wall planners, magnet boards and filing cabinets to create a system that is easy to follow and keep on top of. If you don't, then opt for box files, which you can close and then stack neatly away somewhere at the end of the day, possibly even slotting in under beds and sofas along with your laptop.

With your box files, label them on the outside, for example:

To be actioned
Archived work documents
Payment/Taxes
Current projects

And so on. Three or four should be perfect to get you started. Use these to also store any stationery you have, as well as your paper clips, pens, stapler, etc. This way, it all stays together and you don't have the risk of a little one coming along and playing with your highlighters or a housemate moving round important documents.

Wastepaper bin

You will need somewhere convenient and close by to put your rubbish. Make a point of clearing this once a day so it does not build up.

Decorate your space

Simply put, your workspace needs to be somewhere you are happy to spend time. If you have your own office, make sure it's decorated and clean, add in a few potted plants and colour pictures to make it feel happy and positive, the same as you might do in an office. If you don't have that space, add a few little extras to the space you are working in: a few pictures, colour-coordinated stationery and maybe some inspirational boards to give you a sense of purpose.

Clean up

At the end of your working day, spend the last few minutes straightening up your working area. Tidy up documents and open the window for a while to refresh the area. You are not going to want to enter your workspace the next day and be presented with mess. If your workspace isn't in a dedicated room, have a convenient storage box or basket in which to put your notebooks, laptop and other work items – this way you can reclaim your private space at the end of the day.

Workday Self-care Checklist

Separating work from home can be difficult and, these days, nearly impossible. Use the checklist below to get some ideas on how to separate your day into work and home, making sure you make time for yourself in the morning, at lunchtime and in the evening. Just because you work from home, or even if you're going into work but have a high-pressure job, doesn't mean you have to work over lunch or until midnight. Try to fit in at least five of these self-care treats at each point in the day, to make sure you are really looking after yourself even when you are working hard.

Lunchtime

- [ ] Prepare and eat lunch away from your desk
- [ ] Get outside for some fresh air and sunshine for at least 20 minutes
- [ ] Call a friend or family member
- [ ] 10-minute yoga or stretch
- [ ] 5-minute Challenge
- [ ] Gardening or looking after houseplants
- [ ] Go for a walk or run
- [ ] Walk to the shops for an afternoon treat
- [ ] Get creative with some sketching or crafting

Morning

- [ ] Shower
- [ ] Dress in a nice outfit
- [ ] Hot drink
- [ ] Fresh juice
- [ ] Read a book or newspaper
- [ ] Make and eat breakfast
- [ ] Exercise
- [ ] Listen to music or a podcast
- [ ] 5-minute Challenge
- [ ] Meditate
- [ ] Self-affirmations

After work

- [ ] Finish on time!
- [ ] Close down your computer and tidy away your work area
- [ ] Get outside for some exercise for at least 30 minutes
- [ ] 10-minute meditation or relaxation exercise
- [ ] Enjoy a cup of tea or glass of wine in the garden
- [ ] Play with your pet
- [ ] Enjoy a hobby
- [ ] Catch up with family or friends
- [ ] Cook a favourite meal
- [ ] 5-minute Challenge
- [ ] Bath
- [ ] Face mask
- [ ] Do your nails
- [ ] Gratitude journal
- [ ] Put away devices one hour before bed
- [ ] Read before bed

Cleaning playlist

Downtime playlist

....

....

....

....

....

....

....

....

....

....

....

....

....

....

Banish that Clutter

Before you start any new cleaning routine, you have to banish that clutter. Get your rooms organized, so this way when you grab that quick 5, 7 or 10 minutes of cleaning time, you aren't faced with bigger obstacles. Set yourself a how-to plan – and start with clutter zones.

We all have them in our homes, and some rooms have widespread clutter zones filled with paperwork and general bits and pieces. In the kitchen, you might have a drawer filled with old pens that don't work, half-used rolls of sticky tape and other random items you definitely don't need for cooking. The bedroom could have drawers full of clothes that you don't like or no longer fit, and underneath the bed could be a storage place for items that you just don't know what to do with. The bathroom might have surfaces covered in nearly empty toiletries, candles that have burnt down to nothing, and products that you were gifted for Christmas or your birthday and they're not good for your skin type or you don't like the fragrance. Meanwhile, in the hallway, old keys, unused jackets and mismatched smelly shoes are probably piling up and blocking the entrance. The utility room can become a place where broken or difficult-to-categorize items can go to die and the cabinet beneath your sink could be jam-packed with cleaning materials and products.

These all need to be addressed. Your time and space are valuable, and don't need to be filled up with rubbish. Clutter makes it impossible to keep a home clean and tidy – and once it starts to accumulate, it can seem hard to break the habit.

In order to banish those zones, all you need to do is put aside some time dedicated to this, and create a plan of action and a budget.

Create your plan

Below is an example of a Decluttering Plan, along with the room that needs decluttering, the time you will give to the room, the solution you think will work best in order to tidy and store the clutter, and how much budget you will allocate. The final column, budget, is entirely up to you and what you have available – you can find some amazing bargains on eBay or in second-hand shops. You may even already have what you need elsewhere in your home – get out those baskets full of junk, empty them and put them to proper use!

Example Decluttering Plan

Room	Time allocated	Storage solution	Budget/notes
Kitchen	Half a day		£100
		Mini baskets	Store family snacks
		Fridge trays	These help organize foods and make cleaning the fridge quicker
		Cabinet organizers	
		Plate shelf	
		Cutlery tray	
		Spice racks	
		Bakeware organizer	
		Under-sink organizer	
Utility room	One hour		£40
		Shelving	Use the wall space to create extra storage
		Mini baskets	Store dog leads, hats and gloves
		Under-sink storage: large canisters	For laundry products – choose pretty ones that can double as storage for laundry powders and dishwasher tablets

BANISH THAT CLUTTER

Lounge	Two hours	Seagrass baskets	£500 These are neutral, so work well with most décor and are useful for storing throws and magazines
		Floating shelves	These can make a space looked more polished and add valuable storage for books and ornaments
		Strategic coffee table	Choose one that doubles as storage too
Hallway/ entrance area	One hour	Hall bench	£200 Makes a beautiful hallway seat and gives you plenty of storage for shoes, hats, scarves and gloves
		Long Shaker-style peg rail	These hold plenty of handbags, coats and scarves
		Woven baskets	Another clever way to hide shoes
		Umbrella stand	Keeps wet brollies upright and away from other items
Bedroom	Two hours	Stick-on hooks	£150 Stick to the back of your wardrobe door to hang necklaces

	Shoe racks	Keep shoes together and organized
	Drawer dividers	Perfect for underwear and T-shirt drawers
	Storage bags	A home for the duvet that you are not currently using
	Over-the-door storage	Always make use of the back of the door as it can hold a lot winter coats, cardigans or handbags
Bathroom(s) Two hours		£100
	Shower caddy	Perfect place to store the shampoo and body wash you are currently using
	Mirror with storage function	A dual-purpose cabinet mirror is my go-to for storing family medicines
	Slimline storage cabinet	Hide away cleaning products and loo roll while still having them conveniently nearby
	Small plastic storage boxes	Organization for skincare products, make-up, soaps, shampoo, etc
	Over-the-door hooks	Perfect for dressing gowns and towels

Your Decluttering Plan

Room	Time allocated	Storage solution	Budget/notes

Paperwork

The absolute biggest cause of clutter in every busy home is paperwork, and this is the first thing you need to tackle in your decluttering journey. Our paperwork can be so important, and yet we often treat it with very little respect. How will you go on holiday if you can't find your passport, or pay your bills if the latest gas bill goes astray? The postperson pops myriad letters and leaflets through the door, and when you're busy, the pile just gets bigger and bigger until it is somewhat out of control.

Set up a home filing system for all your paperwork

This is quite a big task, but once it's done, it will serve you well, and you will be able to easily locate documents.

Creating a well-organized filing system in your home reduces paper clutter. It will also help you to get a better hold on your finances, and save you time when you need to find important documents like birth certificates and bits and pieces for applications, tax returns and so on. Nobody wants to spend hours scrabbling around trying to find boring bits of paper when you could be doing something more exciting with your time!

A home filing system needs to:

* Be easy to use

* Keep the whole family organized

* Be an approach that will be maintained

Make your home filing system as uncomplicated as possible – that way you can also rely on other members of the household to stick to the system.

You will need the following:

* Filing cabinet or storage unit

* Box files – ideally, have one per person

* Labels – it is important to clearly identify the files

* Permanent marker

* Paper shredder

* Recycling bin

Once you have these items, gather all of your papers from around the home into one spot. Don't just go to the obvious spaces like the home office or the kitchen – look further afield.

For example, shopping bags, schoolbags, handbags and briefcases all have a tendency to accumulate papers. You might also find them under the doormat, on top of the fridge, on the bookshelves, under the sofa – pretty much anywhere they can be left and forgotten about.

Create three piles:

Keep
Relevant documents you need to keep, including tax paperwork, certificates, and medical records.

Recycle
This could include junk mail, takeaway menus, newspapers, magazines, old schoolwork and opened envelopes.

Shred
Documents you don't need any more that contain personal details, such as addresses or other sensitive identifying information. These can be recycled after shredding.

Having all the items to file in one spot will help keep you focused and more thorough. Once you have your "keep" pile, create categories and write labels. Here are a few suggestions:

* Utilities

* Banking

* Credit cards

* Insurances/guarantees

* Medical records

* House deeds/contracts

* Passports/birth certificates

* Qualification certificates and transcripts

* Marriage/civil partnership certificate

* Work contracts and pension information

* Payslips and/or invoices

* Children's schoolwork, certificates and artwork

The list can be endless, but tailor yours to you and your family. Eliminate any categories you personally don't need, or create a special, separate filing system for a category with a multitude of documents.

If you are self-employed or run your own business from home, you need to keep any tax-related information for seven years. Each year should have its own file. This will include all of your work-related receipts, invoices and any documentation from the tax office.

For household bills, I would suggest filing these by year. For less current utility bills, I would recommend storing these digitally instead – you can save a lot of space by scanning them and shredding the hard copies.

Let's face it, we all want to keep every lovely thank-you note from friends and every piece of our child's artwork or schoolwork, but if we did this we would be drowning in paper. Display the notes you cherish most and the works your child is most proud of, respectively, in frames. Scan the rest – you can have a beautiful photo book created of the others, which can be kept tidily on a bookshelf.

Filing paperwork doesn't have to be a tough task. By following these easy steps, you can create and maintain an organized system with ease.

10-minute declutter buster

You may now be thinking, "I seriously cannot declutter my home in 10 minutes – is 10 minutes even worth the effort?" When it comes to decluttering, many people feel the need to dedicate a whole weekend or even an entire week to declutter.

But just like my 5-minute Challenge for cleaning, you will be really surprised at how much you can accomplish in 10 minutes – especially if you choose to focus on just one small area at a time. These little chunks of time can pop up anywhere, so don't forget to multitask if you are on the phone or waiting for something. Use that previously underutilized time to start doing.

Ten minutes is more than enough to make a big dent in your home's cleanliness.

Break down your organizing and decluttering

Say your bathroom is looking like it needs a good declutter, but it needs quite a bit of time to get it right and you're so busy you literally cannot find a big chunk of time to tackle this. Split your bathroom into 10-minute chunks, spread out so they are convenient to your schedule.

10-minute Declutter Buster Checklist

Bedrooms

- [ ] Wardrobe (split this into four blocks of time)
- [ ] Bedroom drawers (one at a time)
- [ ] Under the bed
- [ ] Shoes
- [ ] Surfaces
- [ ] Jewellery
- [ ] Hair tools
- [ ] Skincare products
- [ ] Windowsills
- [ ] Match up socks

Bathrooms

- [ ] Under the sink
- [ ] Cabinet
- [ ] Towels
- [ ] Windowsills
- [ ] Toiletries
- [ ] Cleaning caddy

Lounge

- [ ] Coffee table
- [ ] Bookcase
- [ ] TV cabinet
- [ ] Fireplace
- [ ] Windowsills
- [ ] Stack and store magazines/books
- [ ] Gather your throws/blankets and store neatly

Kitchen

- [ ] Food cupboards
- [ ] Plates
- [ ] Mugs and glasses
- [ ] Cleaning cupboard
- [ ] Laundry cupboard
- [ ] Windowsills
- [ ] Cutlery drawer
- [ ] Tea towels
- [ ] Cleaning cloths
- [ ] Kitchen appliances
- [ ] Bread bin
- [ ] Fridge door (sort any attached receipts/notes/children's artwork)
- [ ] Freezer (label foods)

Hallway

- [ ] Coats and shoes
- [ ] Coat pockets (check for loose change/old receipts)
- [ ] School bags and handbags
- [ ] Loose mail

* Declutter under the sink

* Declutter the bathroom cabinet

* Sort through your bathroom cleaning caddy

* Declutter towels and bathmats

* Declutter beauty products

* Clean make-up brushes

You can actually choose to do one or even two of these tasks when the bath is running.

Then craft the same type of task list for your kitchen, bedrooms, shared spaces, garages, sheds and so on.

When decluttering, try not to get sentimental. We all have items that we do have an emotional connection to, and you do not have to throw them all away, but the goal is to reduce them. Follow my 10-minute Declutter Buster checklist on page 61, put yourself to work and tick the tasks off as you go.

Don't forget to declutter your life, too

Decluttering our lives is often something we forget to do, but it is crucial to declutter our lives beyond possessions.

Make more space for activities and people you love. Evaluate all the people in your life and then remove toxic people and activities that aren't worth your time and energy.

To help you do this, start with the manageable tidy-ups I've included on my Declutter Your Life checklist overleaf – add your own to complete.

Declutter Your Life Checklist

☐ Delete apps from your phone you don't use

☐ Delete old addresses and unwanted contacts in your phone and address book

☐ Purge your social media accounts of people you're not friends with and accounts you don't want to follow any more

☐ Organize your home entertainment – delete shows you have recorded but will not watch, create a My List on Netflix

☐ Organize your social media into just one space, use Hootsuite or similar manager

- ☐ Declutter your computer desktop

- ☐ Donate books you won't read again

- ☐ Unsubscribe from blogs you never read

- ☐ Declutter your inbox

- ☐ Edit your internet bookmarks

- ☐ Unsubscribe from emails you never read

- ☐ Find all your reusable shopping bags, fold into samosas (see next page) and store together

Step-by-step on how to fold your bag into a samosa

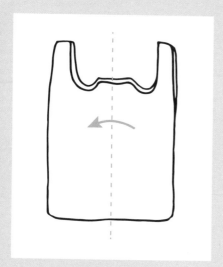

1. Fold the bag in half

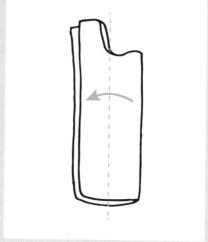

2. Fold it in half again

3. Make sure there is no air trapped in the bag. From the closed end of the bag, fold one corner up to the opposite side, making a small triangle.

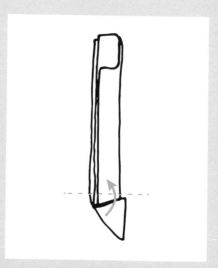

4. Fold the bottom of that triangle up to opposite side, and keep going until you reach the end of the bag.

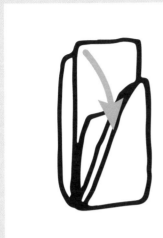 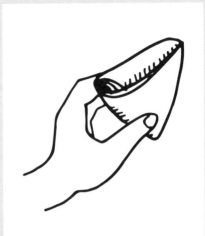

5. When you reach the end, tuck the last bit of bag into your triangle, and you have your bag samosa!

How to be more organized every day

Below are a few ideas to help you with your daily organization, which will help stop the build-up of clutter and save you time. Create your own Daily Organization Checklist using these as inspiration – carry a copy of this or use a small notepad or the notes function on your smartphone, to make sure you won't forget those vital day-to-day tasks.

* Create a daily to-do list

* Leave your house keys and phone in a designated space so you can always find them

* Check your bank balance daily

* Organize your clothes for the following day

* Declutter your purse and handbag weekly

* Meal plan

* Stick to a routine

Daily Organization Checklist

To Do   Done

....   ☐

....   ☐

....   ☐

....   ☐

....   ☐

....   ☐

....   ☐

....   ☐

....   ☐

....   ☐

....   ☐

....   ☐

....   ☐

....   ☐

....   ☐

....   ☐

Speed up home organization with these golden rules

I have a few golden rules when it comes to organizing your home. If you follow these rules, you will find that clutter doesn't build up as quickly, and when (or if) it does, you can implement the 10-minute declutter buster to get back on track.

When I was growing up, my mum always said to me, "Put your stuff away, or it's going in the bin!" This has stuck with me since childhood and I always try to both care for my belongings and put them in their designated place.

Personal clutter is distracting and stressful. It's almost impossible to find items when you need them, and it occupies your mind, keeping you from getting things done. Don't make it harder for yourself to adopt your new daily 15-minute Clean. You need a good base to build upon – and this means a clutter-free home.

Establish a place for everything

You can't really be organized until all of your things have a home. Decide where your tidied and organized items need to go. For example, that massive pile of dirty laundry in the corner of your kid's bedroom doesn't really have a home, so invest in a laundry hamper that fits in with the décor of the room. When the hamper is full, make it their responsibility to bring their dirty clothes to the washing machine.

When working out where to start, don't cheat by shoving everything in the loft or garage – this is self-defeating.

Organize those clutter zones

Once you've thoroughly decluttered your home, you need to come up with a solution to keep it that way; this is essential for when you do your 15-minute Clean. I have popped a few potential problems and solutions here for you.

Problem: loose magazines and newspapers

Solution: The magazine stockpile shouldn't be an issue at all. Boxes and magazine files are a great way to store your magazines, especially because they come in all different sizes and styles for you to choose from and are structured. This structure supports your magazines so that they do not bend and become damaged.

If you want to be able to flip through your magazines easily, then choose a magazine file or a box without a lid, as these attractive options display your favourite magazines while making it easy to take a peek at them. On the other hand, if you are interested in keeping your magazines out of the way, then make sure that you buy boxes that come with lids. These can easily be stored and even stacked on top of one another.

Problem: candles

Solution: Everyone loves candles, but many of them will have different fragrances, and you may not want to burn them all at once and mix all of the scents. Candles do create clutter, so keep out one or two and pop the rest in a drawer until you are ready to burn them. Don't just have them out with no intention to burn.

Problem: the junk drawer

Solution: Let's be honest – we all have one. It is not necessarily a bad thing, because we always have odds and ends that don't really have a home. Don't be ashamed to have one, but use your junk drawer wisely.

A junk drawer does free you up from the pressure of having to be completely organized.

If you can, keep the junk to just one drawer and section it off. Use small drawer organizers, or even cut up old cereal boxes, to create zones within the drawer.

Group items that are often used together or serve similar purposes, such as batteries and light bulbs, scissors and Sellotape, and so on. You could also invest in a small set of drawers with one drawer for each category – then label this up so you'll never be scrabbling around for a safety pin again.

Store like with like

Not only does storing like with like look better, it is also the most practical option. Group items in pairs, like pens and stationery; your pets' bits and pieces; sunglasses, hats and scarves; and so on. These can go in individual storage baskets or boxes and be kept where you will need these items most often, or you can find storage solutions relevant to the items. For accessories, you may want organizers to go inside your wardrobe so you can easily select these when dressing. There are some clever tools out there, including space savers like pockets that hang on the inside of wardrobe doors for easy access.

Adopt a "no freebies" policy for your home

We've all been here before. You attend a conference or festival and come with a ton of free gifts. I mean, who couldn't use a new, free T-shirt, pen, water bottle, or drinks cooler?

It may seem like a good idea at first. But, in reality, it's just more stuff you don't truly need adding to your clutter. While this definitely takes some willpower, especially when the people you are with go freebie crazy, by stopping the stockpiling on all these freebies, you will definitely reduce your household clutter.

Have less stuff

It is much easier to stay organized if you have less stuff. Moving forward, try to only buy what you need and give away or recycle items that you are no longer using. Basically, do not buy anything that doesn't serve a purpose. There may be a sale at your favourite shop, but that does not mean you must rush and buy something that you really don't need. In the same vein, try to avoid "buy one, get one free" offers, as I bet most of the time you don't get a benefit from the deal. Operate a one in, one out policy, giving something to charity or reselling an item every time you buy something new.

Having less stuff does actually give you more freedom; the accumulation of stuff in our homes is a bit like an anchor, tying us down. Let it go and you will experience a freedom like never before.

Declutter routine

Once you are in the habit of putting things where they belong, everything should start clicking into place, so that when you see something out of place, you jump to put it where it belongs. Make sure the rest of your household does the same.

Bathroom Declutter Checklist

We all get products for one reason or another that we just won't use. The most common culprits are items included in boxed sets that we've been gifted for Christmas, free samples, and being swayed by a promotional offer when you pop in to get your shampoo.

The list below should spark some inspiration for what to purge from your bathroom. Next time the bath is running or you are sat in the bathroom waiting for your fake tan to dry, use that time wisely.

Toiletries	If you aren't going to use them, if they are out of date or if you simply hate the smell, then it is time for them to go. Don't forget, many women's refuge centres and some food banks accept unwanted toiletries as long as they are unopened, allowing the products to be redistributed to someone who actually needs and wants them.
Cleaning products	Go through your bathroom cleaning caddy and remove products that you are not using, then re-evaluate where they will work best elsewhere in your home.
Make-up	Check that make-up isn't past its use-by date.
Toothbrushes	Swap every three months.
Bathroom scales	If you don't use it, it just collects dust – off it goes!
Hair dryer accessories	Hair dryers usually come with a lot of accessories that you don't actually use. If you won't, it is time for them to go on the donate pile.
Hairgrips and hair ties	If bent beyond use or unwearable, toss.

Toilet brush	If you use a toilet brush, these do need replacing on a regular basis.
	Cleaning your toilet with a less-than-sanitary brush just moves germs around.
Blunt razor blades	Get rid of these, because life really is too short.
Excess bathroom towels and flannels	How many towels do we really need? Most of us have too many. The rule of thumb with towels is two per person to keep clutter down, plus a bunch of guest towels.
Bathmats	If it doesn't match your bathroom décor or is looking a little tatty, then it is time for these to be recycled.
Kids' bath toys	These can often harbour many germs and be mouldy, check them over and replace if not salvageable. Your kids may have also grown up and no longer play with them – scrub them and give to charity for someone else to enjoy.
Bathroom décor and candles	Burnt-out candles collecting dust need to go, and small bathroom decorations that are just in the way causing clutter need to be tossed as well.
Perfume that is past its prime	If you have had it for years, and it now smells rancid, toss it.

Tip: When you open a new item, check today's date and the recommended amount of months to keep it for – and write that date on the side (a sticker works well). Then, you can easily see when things should be changed.

Kitchen Declutter Checklist

Fifteen items to declutter from your kitchen

The kitchen, I find, is the hub of the family home and can collect the most clutter, so it's always a good starting point to get you fired up to get it in order.

Cleaning cloths	Disregard those that have seen better days — having good cloths makes home cleaning and doing the dishes much more bearable and, in turn, speeds up the process. A cloth full of holes does not clean well.
Tea towels	Stained, out of shape and holey ones can be repurposed for garden work and garage cleaning.
Cookbooks	Donate cookbooks that you no longer use. For books that have in only one or two recipes consider making a copy of the page before you donate the book, and then make a plastic wallet or ring binder of your favourite recipes.
Baking trays	If you have loads and hardly ever use them, it's time for them to go.
Cleaning supplies	Use what you have, stop buying them just because they have a pretty bottle and buy multipurpose products for efficiency. Create a space for cleaning products and try to stick to this space only. Have the bottles that you currently use near the front and use these ones up before you start fresh ones.
Wooden utensils	Are these damaged, or do you have far too many? Then these need to stop clogging up your drawers.

Mixing bowls	If you are not much of a baker, you really don't need a cupboard full of mixing bowls. Choose your favourite and donate the rest.
Worktops	When crammed with clutter, these are hard to keep clean and germ-free. Get rid of unneeded small appliances and keep paperwork to a minimum. Decorative accessories collecting dust and using up space are not really needed in a kitchen space, so re-evaluate where these go.
Dry foods	Check dates on items that are opened, such as rice and pulses, and toss anything you won't be using. Donate in-date items that you don't think you will use to a local food bank.
Tupperware	Match up lids and bottoms and recycle anything that doesn't fit. Donate if you have far too many and won't use them all at once.
Cutlery	Check you have a full set.
Junk drawer	We all have one, but empty it fully and decide what you do and don't need.
Pots and pans	If you can't mend wobbly handles or find missing lids, then these should get the boot.
Mugs and glasses	They say you need two mugs and two glasses per person living in your household.
Kitchen gadgets	Do you have a bread or pasta maker that you have never used? If you haven't used it in the last six months, you don't need it.

Time to Clean

One sentence I hear all the time is "I just haven't got the time to clean". But when I then question this and say, "Why not?" it is always the same excuses: working, looking after the children, too tired and so on, and do you know what – I totally understand. But in all seriousness, you cannot be productive in an untidy home.

You can find the time and with my really simple time challenges you will be so surprised at what you can actually achieve. In just 15 minutes a day, so much can be done. Ask yourself how much time a day you spend scrolling through your social channels on your phone – I bet it will be at least an hour. Yes, you want your social media fix or that bit of TV, but when you are struggling to fit everything in you really are wasting time.

I want you to try my challenges. I know this works as I developed the 5-minute Challenge when I was really struggling for time and it totally changed my outlook on my housework. Combining three of these challenges into a daily 15-minute Clean is my solution to the problem of never having the time to clean. Absolutely everyone can find 15 minutes a day!

All you need is a timer and a little bit of motivation and the rest will come easily. The beauty of this challenge is you can rope your family in too and turn it into a little bit of a family competition. I am so excited for you to get into this habit! Let's get started…

My 5-minute Challenge

Years ago, when I was a single mum of premature twin babies, I had no choice but to be super organized and work quickly – if one baby was happy, the other one wasn't. It was a constant juggling act between numerous hospital appointments, dealing with the local authority due to my circumstances at the time, and having daily healthcare visits. Life was pretty tough, and I didn't have any help around me. My confidence was at an all-time low and my anxiety was through the roof, but cleaning made me happy and kept me going.

The house was always messy, so I needed to fit some sort of structure and plan into my days.

I was not motivated in the slightest, but as time seemed to be so precious, I started to time myself when I was tidying and cleaning the bathroom and realized that actually the housework didn't really take that long. I started at 10 minutes and found myself completing what I wanted in that period, so I moved it down to 5 minutes.

I did this every day around 8 a.m. when the twins went back to sleep for an hour or so, using the quiet to blitz a few rooms, get on top of the laundry and just sit and enjoy a bit of morning TV with a cup of tea – which, believe me, I needed – and I have never looked back.

As my family grew, I continued to use my method and found that my home was always presentable and clean.

All of my friends now live by my 5-minute Challenge – after all, none of us wants to spend a day a week cleaning the house. Anyone who follows me on social media will know that the 5-minute Challenge is the cornerstone of my cleaning philosophy.

Challenge time

I often share my 5-minute Challenge through social media, and it has helped and motivated many people.

The idea is simple: you set your timer on your phone, watch, stopwatch or even your oven (if you are cleaning your kitchen) to just five minutes, and work against the clock. If you are reading this and thinking, "No way is this possible," don't panic. The idea is that this challenge works for you, so adapt the time to suit your needs: try 7, 10 or even 15 minutes. As you get to grips with this new way of cleaning, slowly reduce the time down until you hit 5 minutes. With practice, you can gradually get your time down until you are blitzing your tidying.

It may sound crazy, but trust me – it works wonders. The psychological aspect of working against the clock really does help, and you will be surprised at what you can actually achieve in 5 short minutes.

In that time, you could scroll through your social media, send out a few texts or make a cup of tea – but you can actually achieve so much more when you put your mind to it.

Five minutes is a substantial amount of time, but if you still don't believe me, then up it to 10 minutes and assess the difference.

Your 15-minute Clean

Now that you understand the 5-minute Challenge, it is time to create the perfect cleaning schedule for you and your family by combining three of these challenges every day – your 15-minute Clean.

By blitzing three rooms a day, spending five minutes on each, you will achieve so much more than when you save all your chores up for the weekend. Not only will working against the clock make you speedier and more efficient, but you will have more time to spend on your hobbies, with friends and family, and on valuable self-care.

Choose three rooms a day, for example:

Lounge
Bedroom
Main bathroom

The following day, switch the order of the rooms:

Kitchen
Study
Cloakroom

Keep adding rooms until you have covered your whole home. You may also choose to repeat a few of your high-traffic rooms, such as the main shared bathroom and the kitchen. As long as you are sticking to your daily 15-minute Clean, you will find you are on top of your housework.

The truth is that no one schedule will work perfectly for the same two households. If you have young children, you may find some tasks need to be completed daily to prevent falling behind, and if you live alone, you may find that some tasks only need to be completed once a week. Allergy sufferers may need to vacuum more frequently and messy home cooks may need to disinfect surfaces more often, so make sure to customize your schedule to fit you and your home.

Before you start, you need to plan what you are going to do in each room. Write this down so you know exactly what needs to be done and you won't lose focus.

Creating your cleaning plan

Below I have outlined a variety of 5-minute Challenges, plus the products you'll need to complete them, from which you will be able to build your own personalized cleaning plan. There are also some 15-minute Challenges for those days when you have one room that needs particular attention – on these days, spend the whole of your 15-minute Clean in one room, giving it a good deep clean. If you have 5 minutes here, 5 minutes there and 5 minutes before bed, you can spread your three 5-minute Challenges across the day to complete your 15-minute Clean. Over the week, a combination of these tasks will result in a lovely clean house.

Five-minute Challenges	15-minute Challenges (for deeper cleans)
Entrance hall and stairs	**Entrance hall and stairs**
Shake doormat	Shake doormat
Tidy shoes and coats	Tidy shoes and coats
Light dust	Wipe down internal door and door frame
	Vacuum stairs
	Dust
Products needed	
Dry dusting cloth	Dry dusting cloth, damp dusting cloth for door and frame, vacuum
Lounge	**Lounge**
Plump cushions	Plump cushions
Vacuum	Vacuum
Light dust	Dust well
	Clean mirrors and windows
	Dust TV screen

Reach up high for cobwebs
Light fittings
Tidy books and magazines

Products needed
Vacuum, dry duster, fabric refresher

Vacuum, dry duster, long-handled duster, TV screen cloth and fabric refresher

Study
Dust shelves
Dust and clean computer
Vacuum

Study
Dust shelves
Dust computer
Vacuum
Wipe down desk
Vacuum office chair and wipe down
Sanitize phone
Light fixtures
Clean windows
Dust blinds/vacuum curtains

Products needed
Dry dusting cloth and vacuum

Dusting glove, glass cleaner, antibacterial cleaner for the desk and phone, dry dusting cloth, vacuum

Cloakroom
Wipe down toilet
Add in bleach
Wipe down sink basin
Change hand towels

Cloakroom
Deep clean toilet
Wipe down the basin
Polish and clean taps
Clean mirror
Mop floor
Change hand towels
Check hand soap and refill if needed
Check toilet-roll supply

Products needed
Blue cloth for toilet
Toilet bleach or
denture tablet
Pink cloth and
antibacterial spray for sink

Blue cloth for toilet
Toilet Bleach or denture tablet
Glass cleaner for mirror
Pink cloth and antibacterial spray
for sink
Flat-headed mop
Floor-cleaning product

Bedrooms
Put away any stray clothes
Light dust
Vacuum
Open window
Make bed

Bedrooms
Put away any stray clothes
Clear surface clutter
Vacuum (move what furniture
you can)
Open window
Clean window
Make bed
Dust blinds/curtains
Light fittings
Disinfect TV controls
Remove any rubbish

Products needed
Dry dusting cloth
Vacuum

Vacuum
Dusting glove for blinds
Long-handled duster for light
fittings
Glass cleaner for mirrored furniture
and window
Disinfectant spray for TV controls,
light switches and door handle

Other bedrooms
As above

Other bedrooms
As above

Products needed
As above

As above

Bathrooms
Wipe down toilet
Wipe down sink
Wipe down bath/shower
Shake bathmat
Leave window ajar

Products needed
Blue cloth for loo
Pink cloth for sink
Different cloth to clean bath/
shower
Bathroom cleaning product

Bathrooms
Deep clean toilet
Clean sink and polish taps
Clean bath/shower
Change bathmat
Clean bathroom floor
Change towels
Clean mirrors and windows
Mop floor
Wipe light switch

Blue cloth for loo
Toilet cleaning product
Pink cloth for sink
Bathroom cleaning product
Vacuum
Flat-headed mop
Different cloth to clean bath/shower

Kitchen
Wipe down worktop
Vacuum or sweep floor
Clean sink
Switch over cloths and tea towels

Products needed
Pink cloth for surfaces
Antibacterial spray
Vacuum

Kitchen
Wipe down worktop
Wipe down cabinet doors
Clean sink
Take out rubbish and wipe down bin
Clean hob
Wipe inside microwave
Vacuum or sweep floor
Wash floor
Wash window and sill

Pink cloth for surfaces
Antibacterial spray
Vacuum
Cloth to clean bin
Cloth to clean hob
Glass cleaner
Flat-headed mop

Utility/laundry room
Wipe down worktops
Vacuum or sweep floor
Clean sink area

Utility/laundry room
Wipe down worktop
Wipe down cupboard doors
Take stock of laundry products
Remove and clean washing-machine drawer
Tidy any clothes
Vacuum or sweep floor
Clean sink area

Products needed
Pink cloth for surfaces
Antibacterial spray
Vacuum

Pink cloth for surfaces
Antibacterial spray
Vacuum
Flatheaded mop for floors

Don't feel pressurized to do this all in one go, either. Cleaning does not need to be a marathon! Take regular breaks after a round to rest your mind, calm yourself and plan your next round.

Remember, three rooms using the 5-minute Challenge is just 15 minutes of housework a day. Do this in the morning, and then it is out of the way. Don't forget to mix it up and do different rooms on different days.

When you have a day off or a few spare hours at the weekend, that is when you can do an even deeper clean, if needed. Decide at the start how much time you wish to allocate to your deeper clean and stick to it. Remember that working against a clock is the motivation you need to get tasks done.

Quick bursts of cleaning will make a huge difference to how your run your home and reward you with spare time. Cleaning fast will also help with your fitness and health, so turn your housework into your workout. I, for one, struggle to find the time to go to the gym or see a personal trainer, so cleaning is my fitness. After completing your 15-minute Clean, your heart rate will be racing.

Your 30-day Plan

Use the templates on the following pages to make a quick cleaning plan for the next 30 days. You'll be amazed at the change in your home after only a few short weeks of speed cleaning every day. You'll also learn what tasks your particular home needs more or less of, or if there are areas where you need to set aside time for a declutter so you can do your speed cleaning.

Make a note on each day which area you are going to tackle. If you are sticking to 5-minute Challenges, choose three of these per day – distribute some 15-minute Cleans throughout so that the areas that need more attention are getting it.

There are huge benefits to having a quick cleaning routine

Cleaning quickly (and often) is effective and does not have to be complicated.

You may not want to clean your house daily because it seems like such a lot of effort and possibly a waste of time, but in the long run it will save you time and give you a more organized and tidier place to live.

Remember: it is much easier to clean a contained mess than a home overflowing with clutter. Your newfound benefits include:

1) You can find things

When you maintain a clean and organized home, locating an item you need is painless. Plus, it allows you to see what you have, which will hopefully stop any repeat or unnecessary purchases.

2) Your home is consistently presentable

When one of your friends texts and tells you they are popping in, you will not have to do the panic clean – or open up a cupboard and chuck everything in – just to make your home look presentable. Speed cleaning will enable you to not feel embarrassed about your home and ready and happy to invite people in.

3) You may be happier

A clean, tidy house can make a huge difference to your mood, reducing stress and boosting positive feelings. It's much more pleasant to enjoy your morning cuppa in a clean kitchen that does not have yesterday's mess. You'll have loads more time to relax and enjoy some self-care now that you're not spending the whole weekend cleaning!

4) You can ask for help

If your home looks as though a tornado has just swept through it, then no one is going to have any desire to help you. They will see it as a huge challenge and just shy away. But by utilizing small, regular cleans, the mess is more manageable. Just imagine if you were presented with one week's laundry – it will be enough to put anyone off – but doing a load a day keeps everything attainable. If you live alone, don't be afraid to ask friends for help, especially with those bigger jobs that need more than one pair of hands – make a fun day of it.

Don't forget seasonal tasks

Seasonal tasks tend to be the most forgotten cleaning tasks, because our attention is only needed in these areas two or three times a year. Though infrequent, these are critical to refresh your home. Never fear: most can be done in a short amount of time.

Getting started

Use the clock below to think about your top priorities for your 5-minute Challenges
– out of all of the possible tasks to be completed, what do you see as most important
for your home? Which areas need most attention and are you keen to get stuck into?
These are the challenges you should tackle first when you get started with your daily
15-minute Clean. Remember, the ultimate goal of your 15-minute Clean is to have
more time for you – whether that's time for a cup of tea and a book, or more time
with friends and family, it's priceless.

30-day Plan

1

- [ ] ....
- [ ] ....
- [ ] ....
- [ ] ....
- [ ] ....
- [ ] ....
- [ ] ....

....
....
....
....
....
....
....
....
....
....
....
....

2

- [ ] ....
- [ ] ....
- [ ] ....
- [ ] ....
- [ ] ....
- [ ] ....
- [ ] ....

....
....
....
....
....
....
....
....
....
....
....
....

3

- [ ] ....
- [ ] ....
- [ ] ....
- [ ] ....
- [ ] ....
- [ ] ....
- [ ] ....

....
....
....
....
....
....
....
....
....
....
....
....

4

- ☐ ....
- ☐ ....
- ☐ ....
- ☐ ....
- ☐ ....
- ☐ ....
- ☐ ....

....
....
....
....
....
....
....
....
....
....
....
....

5

- ☐ ....
- ☐ ....
- ☐ ....
- ☐ ....
- ☐ ....
- ☐ ....
- ☐ ....

....
....
....
....
....
....
....
....
....
....
....
....

6

- ☐ ....
- ☐ ....
- ☐ ....
- ☐ ....

....
....
....

7

- ☐ ....
- ☐ ....
- ☐ ....
- ☐ ....

....
....
....

30-day Plan

8

- [ ] ....
- [ ] ....
- [ ] ....
- [ ] ....
- [ ] ....
- [ ] ....
- [ ] ....

9

- [ ] ....
- [ ] ....
- [ ] ....
- [ ] ....
- [ ] ....
- [ ] ....
- [ ] ....

10

- [ ] ....
- [ ] ....
- [ ] ....
- [ ] ....
- [ ] ....
- [ ] ....
- [ ] ....

11

- ☐ ....
- ☐ ....
- ☐ ....
- ☐ ....
- ☐ ....
- ☐ ....
- ☐ ....

12

- ☐ ....
- ☐ ....
- ☐ ....
- ☐ ....
- ☐ ....
- ☐ ....
- ☐ ....

13

- ☐ ....
- ☐ ....
- ☐ ....
- ☐ ....

14

- ☐ ....
- ☐ ....
- ☐ ....
- ☐ ....

30-day Plan

15

- ☐ ....
- ☐ ....
- ☐ ....
- ☐ ....
- ☐ ....
- ☐ ....
- ☐ ....

16

- ☐ ....
- ☐ ....
- ☐ ....
- ☐ ....
- ☐ ....
- ☐ ....
- ☐ ....

17

- ☐ ....
- ☐ ....
- ☐ ....
- ☐ ....
- ☐ ....
- ☐ ....
- ☐ ....

18

- [ ] ....
- [ ] ....
- [ ] ....
- [ ] ....
- [ ] ....
- [ ] ....
- [ ] ....
....
....
....
....
....
....
....
....
....
....
....
....

19

- [ ] ....
- [ ] ....
- [ ] ....
- [ ] ....
- [ ] ....
- [ ] ....
- [ ] ....
....
....
....
....
....
....
....
....
....
....
....
....

20

- [ ] ....
- [ ] ....
- [ ] ....
- [ ] ....
....
....
....

21

- [ ] ....
- [ ] ....
- [ ] ....
- [ ] ....
....
....
....

30-day Plan

22

- [ ] ....
- [ ] ....
- [ ] ....
- [ ] ....
- [ ] ....
- [ ] ....
- [ ] ....

....
....
....
....
....
....
....
....
....
....
....

23

- [ ] ....
- [ ] ....
- [ ] ....
- [ ] ....
- [ ] ....
- [ ] ....
- [ ] ....

....
....
....
....
....
....
....
....
....
....
....

24

- [ ] ....
- [ ] ....
- [ ] ....
- [ ] ....
- [ ] ....
- [ ] ....
- [ ] ....

....
....
....
....
....
....
....
....
....
....
....

25

- ☐ ....
- ☐ ....
- ☐ ....
- ☐ ....
- ....
- ....
- ....
- ....
- ....

26

- ☐ ....
- ☐ ....
- ☐ ....
- ☐ ....
- ....
- ....
- ....
- ....
- ....

27

- ☐ ....
- ☐ ....
- ☐ ....
- ☐ ....
- ....
- ....
- ....
- ....
- ....

28

- ☐ ....
- ☐ ....
- ☐ ....
- ☐ ....
- ....
- ....
- ....
- ....

29

- ☐ ....
- ☐ ....
- ☐ ....
- ☐ ....
- ....
- ....
- ....
- ....

30

- ☐ ....
- ☐ ....
- ☐ ....
- ☐ ....
- ....
- ....
- ....
- ....

Seasonal Tasks Checklist

- ☐ Pick up leaves from garden – 5 minutes
- ☐ Change over duvet to match the season – 10 minutes
- ☐ Cutting the grass – 15 minutes
- ☐ Flip mattress – 5 minutes
- ☐ Vacuum mattress – 5 minutes
- ☐ Remove mattress and pillow protectors – 5 minutes to remove and 5 minutes to put back on
- ☐ Wash cushion covers and throws – 5 minutes to strip and 5 minutes to put back
- ☐ Wardrobe transition – longer task
- ☐ Defrost freezer – longer task
- ☐ Descale kettle – 10 minutes
- ☐ Organize food cupboards (do one a day) – 10 minutes
- ☐ Clean curtain poles – 5 minutes
- ☐ Dust light bulbs – 10 minutes

- ☐ Clean lampshades – 10 minutes
- ☐ Switch over candles and wax melts to match the season – 10 minutes
- ☐ Clean oven – longer task
- ☐ Clean carpets – longer task
- ☐ Soak cooker filter – 5 minutes
- ☐ Clean garden furniture – 15 minutes
- ☐ Store away winter boots and coats – 10 minutes
- ☐ Safety check household alarm – 5 minutes
- ☐ Clear all air vents of dust – 10 minutes
- ☐ Sweep out garage – 10 minutes
- ☐ Wash shower curtain – 5 minutes to take down and 5 minutes to put back up
- ☐ Clean washing machine – 5 minutes
- ☐ Clean dishwasher – 5 minutes

TWO THOUSAND AND TWENTY ONE

JAN FEB MAR APR MAY JUN JUL AUG SEP OCT NOV DEC

Seasonal To-do Lists

Use this space to create your own
personalized to-do lists for each season.

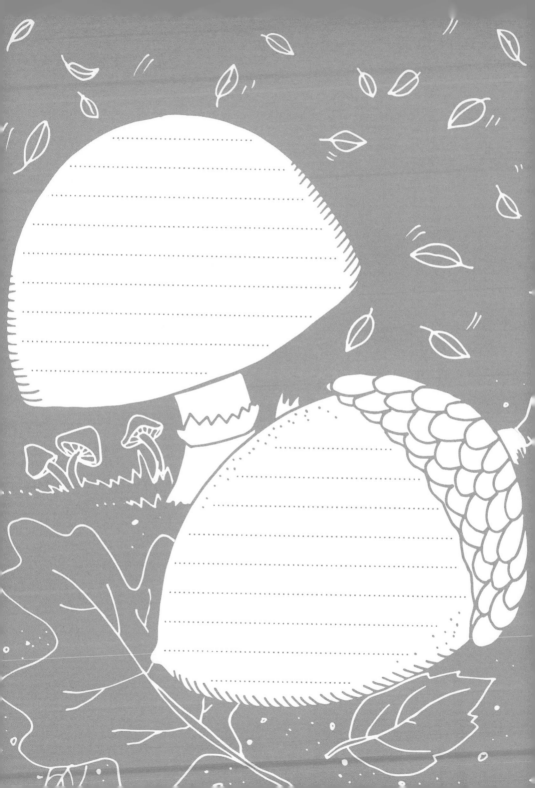

Big clean-ups

Seasonal deep cleans

Your home will need a more thorough deep clean about four times a year. I work mine in seasonally:

Spring clean (late March)
As the weather gets warmer, it's time to throw open the windows and reinvigorate your home after the doldrums of winter.

Autumn clean (September)
After the summer holidays, your home is going to be crying out for some detailed attention.

Christmas clean (early December)
This is the perfect time to start to get ready for guests and the festive season.

New Year clean (January)
On the face of it, this may seem quite soon after your Christmas clean, but in that time your home will have had a lot more traffic and inevitably picked up clutter. Prepare to move into the new year clutter free, with a fresh space to hunker down in for the remainder of the cold weather.

Cleaning zones

An efficient way to tackle these bigger seasonal cleans that are going to take a lot more time is to divide your home up into cleaning zones. No matter the size of your space, delineating zones makes the task at hand far less overwhelming.

When deciding how to assign cleaning zones, think of your home as a cake and cut it into four slices, as on page 115. Each slice, or zone, will contain several layers, or rooms.

Once divided, assign each zone a day. If time allows, do a zone a day over the period of one week. Try to only spend 30 minutes on each zone. Stick to the schedule you have created and aim to get the zones in order as quickly as possible. If you have a larger home, you may need to assign six zones and do them over a longer period of time.

The key is to make this task manageable for you, so if it all looks too much when you plan and write it down, abandon it and start again. If you create an unrealistic plan, you're setting yourself up to fail. Make it easy on yourself and keep your goals attainable.

Once you've got all of these zones back into shape, return to your daily 15-minute Clean plan. Zone ideas could be:

Zone 1
Kitchen
Utility room
Home office
Entrance hall

Dining room

Zone 3
Bedroom(s)
Main bathroom

Zone 2
Lounge
Cloakroom

Zone 4
Bedroom(s)
Bathroom

You can take it a step further – when you are in the bathroom, for example, split that zone again into four sections and tick them off as you go.

Bathroom cabinets
Bath and tiles

Shower and tiles
Toilet and sink

Then, for the bedroom:

Vacuum
Dust furniture

Dressing table
Window area

And so on, breaking it down to make it feel less of a chore.

Create your own zones

Use the cake below to organize the
rooms in your own house into zones.

Additional zones

Zones can also encompass internal and external storage spaces. Be sure to include areas like hallway, under-stair and airing cupboards, wardrobes, garden shed, garage, greenhouse, outhouse, and garden storage box.

The beauty of breaking your home up into zones and following a system for your seasonal deep cleans is that your home will never really get too dirty, so that when you do a big clean at Christmas or in the spring, it will be much smoother sailing than if you have only been doing bits here and there.

The first time using the zone method will be the hardest as your home will be needing a deep clean of each zone, but the second time will be easier because you will have tackled that area recently and there will be much less to do.

Plan and write down what you want to do. This way, you won't forget anything, and you will stick to it.

Alternative plan

Why not build your deep seasonal clean from a selection of 5-minute Challenges? Once you've selected your zone for the day, spend just 5 minutes on each area. For example, if Zone 1 contains your bathroom and bedroom, spend 5 minutes on each – and that's just 10 minutes of housework you've got to complete that day. As I've said before, although I call this the 5-minute Challenge, you can adapt the time to suit you. Five, 10 or 15 minutes – the choice is yours, whatever works for you, and over time you can work your way down to 5 minutes.

The next day, do Zone 2 – this could be your kitchen, utility room, entrance hall and home office – spend 5 minutes on each, a total of just 20 minutes of housework.

Cleaning Zone Planner

	Monday	Tuesday	Wednesday
Zone 1			
Zone 2			
Zone 3			
Zone 4			

Notes

Plan your seasonal deep cleans with my Cleaning Zone Planner. On each day, make a note on the areas of each zone you plan to work on, and tick them off as you finish.

Thursday	Friday	Saturday	Sunday

Notes

Keep fit with cleaning

Did you know that you can increase the number of calories you burn cleaning your home?

If you're having trouble motivating yourself to scrub the bath or give the windows a clean, you might want to think about the calories you'll work off and the muscles you'll tone.

Adding in exercise to your cleaning is easy to do with just a few simple changes to your cleaning routine. Most household chores burn calories using some of the same physical movements that you do in the gym. With a few small adjustments, you can get a full-body workout, build muscle, and burn calories while you tidy up and clean your home.

Sound good? Grab your rubber gloves, ditch the gym and start cleaning!

Drop some lunges into your vacuuming

Believe it or not, vacuuming makes for an effective tummy toner, but try stepping to a full lunge each time you reach the vacuum (or mop) forward. Bring the legs back together when you pull the vacuum or mop back.

A lunge uses most of the major muscles in your lower body. You also engage the abdominal muscles to help you balance while moving in and out of your lunge.

Stretch and use circular motions when you are cleaning your windows

Window cleaning works the biceps, triceps and shoulders, helping to tone the upper arms and banish bingo wings. Reaching for the uppermost parts of the window on your tiptoes also engages your calf muscles.

Add ankle and wrist weights

Strap on a few weights while you are cleaning to help tone your body. Start with light weights and build up as you get stronger.

Put your shoulders into cleaning the oven

Cleaning a greasy oven is not the nicest of household tasks, and one we try to put off for as long as we can. It can be a gruelling task, but the scouring action you make when you really give it some welly tones the muscles in the shoulder and helps strengthen the wrists, too. If you can, try to be ambidextrous and use both hands for a more balanced workout.

Pick things up off the floor by squatting

When you are picking up anything from the floor, add in a few squats. You may feel a bit silly, especially if someone else is in the room, but this exercise really benefits your glutes.

Take several trips up the stairs

If you have laundry to put away, don't take it all in one go – split the laundry into rooms and make several trips. Going up and down the stairs is a good aerobic exercise and will help to start to shape your buttocks.

Get gardening

Don't forget those naturally fitness-focused tasks that need doing in the garden, such as:

* Raking the leaves
* Trimming hedges
* Weeding
* Digging
* Mowing the lawn

Step Chart

Keep a note of the steps you take and the calories you burn while doing different activities. Challenge yourself to increase your step

Cleaning activity	Steps	Calories burned

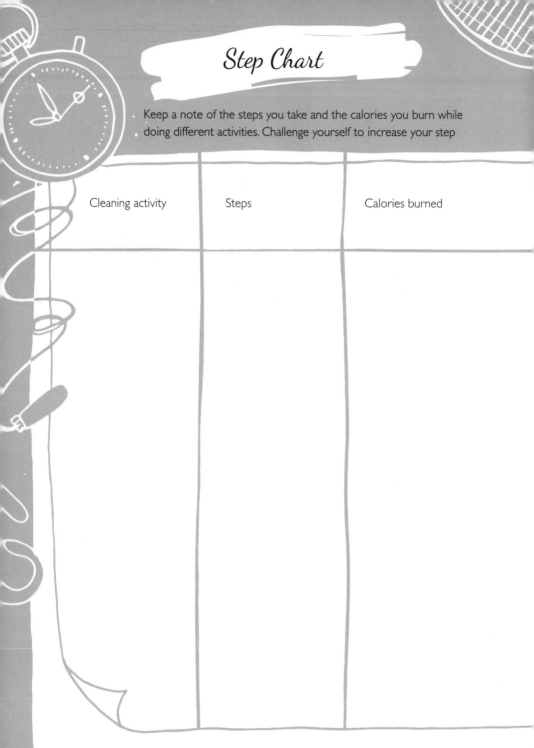

count by really going for it when you're cleaning and giving yourself extra chores to do to reach your daily target. If you're new to doing lots of exercise or have any health issues, always double check with your doctor before starting anything different to your usual routine.

Cleaning activity	Steps	Calories burned

Looking after your home is definitely already a workout, but with these additions you can hit two birds with one stone. Put these tips into practice and if you find it manageable, keep it consistent! The more you do these exercises, the more likely they will turn into a habit. Depending on your weight and height, you can burn over 200 calories with just one hour of housework.

Track your step count when you're cleaning as well, and I think you will be pleasantly surprised at how many you actually do. This may then give you some added motivation to get your vacuum out for a win-win for your home and your body.

Cleaning tips and solutions

Cleaning pillows

Many of us overlook cleaning our pillows and duvets but these items certainly do need cleaning a few times a year.

Pillows collect bacteria, dust, dead skin, dust mites and sweat, and can end up smelling unpleasant or with big yellowish stains.

Here's a discomfiting statistic: up to a third of the weight of your pillow after six months of use could be made up of dead skin and dust mites.

Using thick, quilted pillow protectors helps protect your pillow and if you wash these a few times a month, it certainly helps keep the build-up at bay.

With this is mind, make sure you add pillow cleaning into your schedule. Your pillows will last longer if you give them a little TLC, and they will keep you healthier, too.

These days, many pillows are actually machine washable, which is a fantastic development – the downside is that only one is likely to fit into your washing machine drum at a time.

When the time comes to clean your pillow, you firstly need to know the type of pillow filling you have. This helps you decide the best way to clean it. Check the pillow care label for this information.

If you really don't fancy washing your pillows, a really quick solution is to pop a pillow at a time into your tumble dryer at the hottest heat for 15 minutes. The heat from the tumble dryer will kill off some germs and bacteria.

How to wash your pillows

Feather pillows
Feather pillows can go in the washing machine. Opt for a gentle or delicate wash and spin cycle and add a liquid detergent. If they have yellow staining, then add in a stain remover or a big spoonful of bicarbonate of soda.

To dry, tumble dry on a low setting for a few hours. Add in a few dryer balls or tennis balls to help break up any lumps and to keep them nice and fluffy.

If you don't have a tumble dryer, choose a warm, sunny day to wash your pillows and then lay them flat in the sunshine to dry. Go outside and turn them every hour until they are fully dry.

Foam pillows
Step away from the washing machine – if you wash these you will ruin them. Instead, every so often, use your vacuum nozzle and give them a good clean to remove as much dust, dead skin cells and dust mites as you can. Then spot clean your pillows using a damp cloth with a drop of laundry detergent or upholstery cleaner.

You can put these in the tumble dryer or lay them flat outside in the sun.

When is the time to buy new pillows?

There is a simple test you can do to see if your pillows need replacing. Fold your pillow in half, and if it doesn't pop right back open, then it is time to replace it. This rule, however, doesn't tend to work for foam pillows.

You should also replace your pillow if you notice any really bad odours or if mould and mildew are present.

How to wash your duvet

Again, check your care label, but most of them are machine washable.

If you are lucky and have a good-sized washing machine drum, most duvets fit in for a great deep clean. If you don't, then make use of your local dry cleaners – most offer a duvet-cleaning service at an affordable price.

Just as with the pillows, keeping your duvet clean will extend its life.

When washing in your washing machine, use the lowest setting you can and use a low spin cycle. Shake it really well when you take the duvet out and try and air dry by putting it over your washing line. On a day with good weather, your duvet will dry quickly.

In between washes on a temperate day, hang your duvet outside in the fresh air. This refreshes it and reduces odour build-up.

Cleaning versus disinfecting

There are three main benchmarks use you can opt for when removing dirt, grime and bacteria from a surface in your home, and they are:

Cleaning
Sanitizing
Disinfecting

Each one of these is slightly different, so it's worth taking the time to understand what those differences are.

What is cleaning?

Strange question for a cleaning book, but it's important to understand the distinction!

Cleaning is the process of physically removing visible dirt, grime, dust and debris from surfaces, carpets and floors.

Cleaning does not include tidying up, decluttering or organizing.

When you buy cleaning products, these usually contain fragrance, soap and a detergent. The detergent here is what actually lifts dirt from the surface, allowing you to clean and remove with a good microfibre cleaning cloth. Cleaning does not kill germs.

What is sanitizing?

The main goal of sanitization is to eliminate pathogens, which are microorganisms that can cause disease. Sanitizing a surface reduces some, but not all, of the total number of germs present. This process is particularly important to complete in food preparation areas, to avoid making people sick.

Sanitizing usually occurs after the cleaning process and is achieved using heat and water, strong chemicals or a combination of both. Using a steam cleaner is a fantastic way to lift and kill bacteria all around your home.

What is disinfecting?

Unlike sanitizing, disinfecting isn't just about eliminating pathogens. The ultimate goal is to kill all microorganisms that are present on a surface. Disinfecting is particularly important if an illness comes into your home, and in places like hospitals, where the spread of infection can be rapid.

Because they cannot break through soiling on surfaces, disinfectants need to be used after cleaning agents.

This process can be achieved using a disinfectant spray or wipes, bleach solutions, alcohol solutions, or UV disinfectant lights. This germicidal ultraviolet light breaks up the DNA of germs, making them incapable of reproducing.

Should you clean, sanitize, or disinfect?

Now that we are all on the same page as to what cleaning, sanitizing, and disinfecting are, we can explore when it makes sense to use each method around the home or workplace.

Cleaning daily

Cleaning should be done most frequently, as often as every day, according to your needs and the amount of activity in your house. Basic housekeeping, such as dusting, wiping surfaces clean and vacuuming, helps slow the growth of harmful pathogens and keeps your home orderly and polished.

Cleaning should always come first, even if you ultimately want to sanitize or disinfect something. Sanitizers and disinfectants can't do their jobs well when they are applied to dirty surfaces. So, it is essential to wipe away the grime before using those products.

Sanitize and disinfect frequently

Sanitizing and disinfecting certain surfaces help keep your home healthy and hygienic. Think of those high-traffic areas – where car keys and mobile phones are put down – that take a lot of touch as people come home. These are the areas that will need more than just cleaning. Use a two-step process of cleaning and disinfecting on these frequently touched surfaces in your home daily. Don't forget your kitchen worktops, doorknobs, light switches, and toilets.

When spraying a product to a surface, don't just spray and wipe, but spray and leave for a few minutes to allow the product to actually work and kill germs. Cleaning can help keep your family healthy, but if someone in your home does get sick, it is vital to disinfect. Always use caution with strong products, and read the label and follow instructions.

The two-step cleaning process
Start by removing the visible dirt and any loose debris from the surface, floor or object. Clean the area well using a detergent-based product and a wet microfibre cloth.

Once you have cleaned the area and you are happy you have removed any little bits, apply a disinfectant to the surface and then make sure you leave the product for a few minutes to let it work. The surface should still be wet from the cleaning process; if it has dried slightly, dampen it again.

Magic erasers

Magic erasers deserve a place in everyone's cleaning caddy. They are a quick cleaning solution for removing stubborn grime and scuff marks, and will bring up your walls, surfaces and trainers like new.

How to get the best out of your magic eraser
1) They are quite big and you probably only need a small amount to tackle that quick cleaning job, so cut your magic eraser into pieces. I normally cut mine into chunks of six, so they last longer and you get your money's worth.

2) Before you use your magic eraser, you need to make sure it is damp with either hot or cold water – and then let the magic happen. You do not need to use any product at all.

3) Protect your hands. Magic erasers can be quite coarse, and can irritate your hands when you're scrubbing, so you might want to wear a pair of cleaning gloves to give you that added protection.

What to use your magic eraser for:
Cleaning your hair tools
Hair tools tend to get grimy over time with a build-up of product and hair oils. You can use a magic eraser to restore them back to their former glory and bring that perfect shine back to your hair.

Removing scuff marks
I find that where my patent shoes tend to rub against each other, little black marks can appear. These can normally be tough to remove, but use your magic eraser to clean these marks off with ease.

Whitening trainers
The white rim on trainers is usually the dirtiest part, and can ruin the whole look of your outfit. Using a magic eraser is much better than any chemically abrasive products on your trainers as they can discolour the leather.

Removing permanent marker
If you label plastic food containers with permanent marker, you will know how hard this is to remove, if possible at all. Magic erasers remove pen marks with ease, allowing you to relabel your leftovers clearly.

Removing Sellotape marks
Party decorations popped up over your home using Sellotape can sometimes leave a mark.

Sticker marks
Children can sometimes go a little wild, leaving you with sticker marks on glass windows and doors. If you don't spot this soon enough, these stickers can be a real pain to remove.

Clean up your phone case
Magic erasers make the perfect tool for cleaning up those marks off your phone case, making it look brand new.

Sorting out nail polish remover
I'll never forget that once when I was young, I spilt a whole bottle of nail polish remover on my mum's brand-new table. She scrubbed and scrubbed, and it never quite came out! But the eraser can handle both spills of nail polish and of its remover.

Cleaning those pot bottoms
If you turn over your pots and pans, you may see a few scuff marks from being placed on and off the hob.

Tidy up the microwave
Deal with those quick microwave spillages using a magic eraser to wipe down the inside surfaces.

Make glass shine
If you have a pet, you know how much they love to sit and look out of the window. Occasionally, they leave pet marks on glass. A quick wipe with a magic eraser does the trick, and is much quicker than using a glass cleaner.

Ten ways to clean with eucalyptus oil

These days, many of us are leaning towards using more natural products around our homes. There are many reasons why, including allergies, reactions to chemical products and wanting to protect our environment.

Eucalyptus oil is one of my favourite essential oils to use around my home. The beauty of eucalyptus oil is it is inexpensive and readily available. I love it because it's a bit of an all-rounder and has amazing properties for cleaning: it is antifungal, antibacterial, antiviral and a great deodorizer.

1. Grease buster
Eucalyptus oil is an amazing grease buster and will remove grease and grime from your hob. Just add four drops of eucalyptus oil to a spray bottle of water, add a drop of washing-up liquid, and vigorously shake. This will clean up your extractor fan hood, microwave, oven and your kitchen surfaces, even shining up the kitchen sink.

2. Stain remover
This versatile oil also banishes those greasy stains from car oil, cooking oils, moisturizers and sun creams. All you need to do is coat the stain in the oil, leave it for five minutes to allow the oil to work, and then just add to your wash as normal.

3. Air freshener
Fill a spray bottle halfway with water and then add in a teaspoon of vodka along with 10 drops of eucalyptus oil to make a lovely air freshener.

4. Toilet cleaner
Add a few drops of eucalyptus oil to your toilet bowl and then scrub with a toilet brush. You can also wipe the toilet seat and handle with a drop of oil applied directly with a cloth.

5. Floor cleaner
Add a capful to one litre of hot water to clean and shine up your hard floors.

6. Anti-moth and anti-silverfish treatment
Banish moths and silverfish from your cupboards – wipe neat eucalyptus oil on the inside walls of the cupboard or add a drop of the oil onto a padded coat hanger.

7. Insect deterrent
Wipe down those areas where insects come into your home or put a few drops onto cotton pads and balls and leave these in the areas they tend to enter. Hide the cotton in corners and plant pots.

8. Sticker remover
Eucalyptus oil can be used neat to remove stickers and sticker residue from glass.

9. Mould and mildew
Add a few drops of oil to hot water in a cup and then pour over areas that have been affected by mould and mildew in your bathroom and fridge.

10. Dust mites
Add a few drops of eucalyptus oil to the cycle when you are washing your bed linen, blankets and pillows.

Note: Don't use eucalyptus oil if you are pregnant, and don't use directly around children or animals.

Use your dishwasher's full potential!

As a busy working mum of three kids, I have really had to figure out how to clean most things in my home quickly. But the experience of cleaning up after my kids did teach me so much and one of the most valuable lessons I learned was to make use of what is staring us straight in the face.

Speed up cleaning those awkward, messy items by making good use of your household appliances, such as the dishwasher and the washing machine.

Your dishwasher can actually clean a lot more than just your dishes. There are, of course, some things that you should never put in your dishwasher, such as wooden items and copper.

But when you want to reduce your cleaning time and hassle, then use that magic box in your kitchen and leave it to do the hard work. The following can all be cleaned in the top rack of your dishwasher (read any labels on the item if unsure):

Bath toys
Plastic toys
Lego
Teething rings
Dummies
Kitchen sponges and cloths
Fridge shelves
Cooker hood filters
Hob Toppers
Vases
Bathroom accessories, such as toothbrush holders and soap dishes
Pet food bowls
Baseball caps(they can sit flat so won't lose their shape as they are likely to in a washing machine)

Then there are welly boots and flip-flops, but if you are going to do this, then please ensure you give the dishwasher a good clean afterwards – the soles of our shoes pick up lots of germs.

Washing machines

Don't forget your washing machine too. It certainly isn't just for clothes. Being able to toss things in the washer rather than hand wash individual special items has saved me so much time and effort. But when washing these items, it is important to use a gentle cycle and the correct temperature.

Most washing machines have a "hand wash" option which is perfect for more delicate items. A few examples include:

Soft toys
Backpacks
School lunch bags and soft lunch boxes
Reusable shopping bags
Plastic toys, use mesh laundry bags to keep all the toys together
Oven gloves
Mop heads
Rubber gloves
Shower curtains (if they have any mould patches add in some white vinegar)
Pillows (always dry these flat after washing)
Trainers (I use a heat of 30 degrees Celsius with a liquid detergent that I mix a spoonful of bicarbonate of soda into)
Small rugs
Cushion covers (check the care label, but many wash up well)
Curtains
Net curtains
Car mats
Hair ties and fabric headbands (these can get a build-up of oil and hair products; pop them in a mesh bag)
Pet beds (if they have removable covers, throw those in, too)

Speed
Things Up

Now that you've created your 30-day Plan and worked out those high-traffic areas and clutter zones in your home that need regular attention, it's time to speed things up.

In this chapter you are going to learn how to clean items in your home quickly and efficiently, plus I have listed a whole host of tasks that you can squeeze into your day when you find you have a few minutes spare. When you're waiting to go on the school run, or for the shopping to be delivered, this time can often be wasted. If you use it wisely, it will make a big difference and save you so much time and effort.

Let's not forget learning how to deal with those last-minute guests. You know, the ones that tend to just turn up unannounced with literally just a few minutes' notice! But don't fear. This chapter will have you tackling this situation with great confidence and greeting guests with a spotless home.

Let's get going and speed things up.

Things to clean quickly

Want to speed up some of those awkward jobs in your home?

Follow my speedy cleaning guide, below, for methods and shortcuts to tackle the pitfalls of home life thoroughly and efficiently.

Outdoors

Wellies and walking boots
Winter walks mean one thing: muddy, smelly wellies.

When you are approaching your home, try to knock off as much mud as you can while you walk. Once home, clean the outside with warm, soapy water, scrape off any mud using a blunt knife, and add twisted-up newspaper into the boots to help the inside dry quickly. Leave them like this overnight.

Kids' car seat
Baby and toddler car seats can take quite a beating – enduring everything from spilt drinks and crushed biscuits to vomit and poo explosions – and they can be unpleasant to clean.

Always take the seat out when cleaning – it's easier and saves time.

Grab a handheld vacuum and suck up any loose crumbs, ensuring you get into all the cracks by lifting up the material to get right underneath. Wipe it down using a soapy cloth, spot clean any stains and leave to dry in the sun. If you are lucky enough to have a seat with a cover that lifts off, put this in the washing machine along with any strap covers.

Car upholstery
Keep a lint roller in the glove compartment of your car and use this for quick upholstery tidy-ups for pet hair and crumbs.

BBQ grills
The best, quickest and most eco-friendly way to clean your BBQ is to cut an onion in half, pop it onto the end of a BBQ fork and while the grill is still hot, gently rub the onion up and down to remove grime and food build-up.

Garden plant pots
To clean up your outside garden pots after a heavy winter, use a stiff brush to knock off any built-up soil and debris. Then, using warm, soapy water with a splash of vinegar, clean the rest of the pot and leave to dry naturally.

Plant leaves
Remove dust from plants using a recycled make-up brush and then shine up the leaves using a tiny amount of mayonnaise on your fingers.

Gym/sports clothes cleaning
Don't leave your sweaty sports kit in a bag and then forget about it until next week – act as soon as you get home.

Turn your clothes inside out. Fill a bowl with cold water and add in some white vinegar for a pre-soak. The vinegar helps to break down sweat and neutralize the bacteria that cause smells. After the soak, wash as normal in the machine.

Kitchen

Clean it as it happens
As a general rule, cleaning kitchen appliances becomes much easier if you tackle the mess as it happens, by wiping up spills and as much food residue as possible before it has time to congeal and stick.

Pots, pans and dishes
Scrubbing dirty dishes and cookware can be a back-breaking and time-consuming task. Avoid this by filling your dirty dish or pan with warm water and a few tea bags right before you sit down to your meal. The tannic acid in the tea breaks down the burnt and stuck-on food with ease.

When you have finished your meal, simply pour away the tea and rinse.

Dishwasher

I always remind people to clean the items that clean for them, and the dishwasher is at the forefront of this category. Excess food and grime build up in your dishwasher and mould can grow on the rubber edging. Get into the habit of pulling out the filter once a week, rinsing it under the tap and then running a rinse cycle using either lemon juice or white vinegar in place of the tablet to keep it smelling fresh. A recycled toothbrush is great for the rubber rim – just apply a small amount of washing-up liquid and work around the edging before putting on the rinse cycle.

Microwave

Try to get into the habit of wiping down your microwave after every use. This saves time in the long run, but if your microwave does have a bad odour and some splashes of dried-on food, then try this method: fill a microwave-safe bowl with water and add a few slices of lemon, putting the machine on full power for five minutes. This process will steam up the microwave and loosen all the dried-on food marks. Remove the bowl carefully and then wipe down the insides with a clean cloth.

Plug holes

When you notice your drain is starting to slow or has a bad odour, pour a $\frac{1}{2}$ cup of bicarbonate of soda down it, followed by a $\frac{1}{2}$ cup of white vinegar. This combination fizzes up to break down blockages. Wait five minutes and then flush with hot water.

Kitchen cabinets

You can't see it, but your kitchen cupboards can get really greasy and grimy when you are in full-on Nigella mode. Add a drop of washing-up liquid to a spray bottle with some water and a drop of white vinegar, to clear away the grease and grime plus keep your cupboards streak-free.

Mugs and cups

Drop a denture tablet into your tea- and coffee-stained mugs for a few minutes and your cups will soon be back to sparkling and ready for the next cuppa – no scrubbing required.

Hob

After every use, try and wipe down with a warm, soapy cloth. To get the perfect shine, buff up with a drop of baby oil and a microfibre cloth.

Hob toppers

Hob toppers are often sticky and greasy from frequent cooking. A simple quick tip to keep them clean is to pop them in a sturdy and sealed plastic bag, add in some bicarbonate of soda and a splash of white vinegar, seal and shake the bag. Leave for 10 minutes and then rinse.

Chopping board

Sprinkle your chopping board with some coarse salt, cut a lemon in half, and with the cut side down, scour the surface, squeezing lightly as you go to release the lemon juice. Let this sit for five minutes and then rinse.

Smoothie blender

As soon as you have poured your smoothie into your glass, it's time to clean the unit before it has the chance to become harder work later on. Fill it halfway with warm water and add a drop of washing-up liquid. Put it back on the blending station and give it a quick whizz for 10 seconds. Pour away the water and your blades and blending cup will be all ready for the next smoothie.

Kettle

Water contains minerals and as water boils, some of those minerals get left behind and fall to the bottom of the kettle. This can be problematic if you live in an area with hard water – meaning there are lots of minerals in your water. Over time, these scales, also called "furring", will gunk up the heating element and cause your kettle to be inefficient. Clean your kettle by filling it half with water and half with white vinegar or lemon juice, leaving to sit for 15 minutes, then setting it to boil. After boiling, pour away the solution, refill with water and boil again for a rinse.

Oven trays

Use a paper kitchen towel to wipe up any loose bits, place the tray into your sink and sprinkle it with bicarbonate of soda. Then add boiling water and leave to soak so that any burn marks soften.

Oven

Use an oven liner to soak up cooking spillages, this will save you time when it comes to the big oven clean and these are easy to wipe clean after each use.

Freezer

This one is going to take you a little more time, but for a simple clean, remove all the food into a cool bag or ice box, so it stays frozen. Clean the freezer's interior with a solution of a cup of water mixed with a splash of white vinegar and a spoonful of washing-up liquid. Pop it into a spray bottle and give the freezer a good spray down, wiping it with a sponge afterwards. You can then dry it with paper towels, and refill the freezer with your food.

Fridge

Give the fridge a quick clear-out and basic wipe-down weekly before you go to the shops, so it's ready for the week's groceries. Simply take out fridge shelves and drawers and wipe them down with warm, soapy water.

Children's Lego creations

Children love to be creative with Lego and make imaginative displays in their bedrooms, but these displays really can hang on to dust. Grab an old make-up brush or paintbrush and gently dust the bricks. This is also something you can get your child to do.

Soft toys

Freshen up with a handheld steamer or a lint roller.

Gaming controllers

Using a microfibre cloth with a squirt of disinfectant, clean the entire controller area, ensuring any power sources have been deactivated and unplugged. Use a cotton-wool bud and toothpick to gently clean around the button and joysticks. This will remove any lodged grime.

Mobile phones/tablets

Rubbing alcohol is one of the best products you can use to clean your mobile phone or tablet. Apply the solution to a clean, dry microfibre cloth and rub all over your device. Better still, if you have a UV sterilization machine, pop your phone in for three minutes and use this time to crack on with another cleaning task.

Lounge/family area

Marks on walls
Magic erasers are great at jumping on those pesky wall marks quickly, and with a gentle rub will soon vanish. Alternatively, dampen a sponge, dip into a bowl of bicarbonate of soda and gently rub on the wall marks.

Radiators
If you are lucky enough to own a handheld steamer, this is the perfect tool for releasing dust build-up inside radiators. Simply blast the steamer and watch dust fall within seconds. Alternatively, grab a thin duster and poke it in the gaps, wipe down the front with a warm, soapy cloth and then buff dry.

Ceilings
Flip your flat-headed floor mop upside down, and using a dry pad, lift up and glide it along your ceiling. If you are using a microfibre pad, the dust will stick to the pad rather than fall onto the floor.

Scoop up pet hair
After you have finished doing the dishes, don't remove your damp gloves. Take a detour through the living room and quickly pick up errant pet hair from your sofa or rug.

TV controls
First, remove the batteries from the remote, then use a disinfectant spray and cloth to sweep over the surface a few times. To clean around the buttons, use a cotton-wool bud and a toothpick to remove any stuck debris.

TV screens
No matter what type of television you have, you'll need a dry microfibre cloth that's designed to clean and remove smudges. Spot-clean stubborn smudges with a wipe designed for electronics.

Suitcases
When you come back from holiday, your suitcase is often filled with dirty clothes and towels. After emptying it, go over it with a warm, soapy water solution, paying attention to the wheels and handle. Dry off and then add

in a few tumble-dryer sheets so that next time you prepare to go away, your case is smelling lovely and fresh.

Candle containers
Some candles come in the prettiest containers and it is such a shame to just throw them away when they can help organize or hold something other than candles. Save yours – fill them with boiling water, let sit for a few minutes, watch the unused wax rise to the top and then scoop out the wax with a paper towel.

Ironing
Speed this up by ironing clothes when they are slightly damp, and place on a hanger straight away. This shaves a good few minutes off your ironing time.

Sofa clean
For a rapid sofa refresh, take a damp microfibre cloth and work up and down in strips on your sofa; the microfibre will pick up any loose debris and remove any surface dirt.

Straighten and square
Don't underestimate the impact that taking a minute or two to fluff cushions, fold throw blankets and straighten decorative pillows can have on the look of your living room. Similarly, squaring up stacks of magazines and books is a fast and easy way to create the appearance of a tidy space. A quick pass of the feather duster over bookshelves and coffee tables will help get rid of dust with little fuss; microfibre cloths eliminate fingerprints and smudges in a flash.

Internal doors
A damp microfibre cloth is sufficient enough to keep your internal doors clean and dust free. Dampen one, wipe the door all over and then buff dry using a dry microfibre cloth.

Door handles
One of the most-touched items in your home – keep these clean by spraying a product directly onto a microfibre cloth and then rub it over the handle. Never spray directly onto your door handle as this can discolour the paintwork that surrounds the handle.

Door frames

Always start at the top when you are cleaning your door frames, as dust will fall like snow. Dust the top of the door frame using a slightly damp cloth and continue around. If your frame feels sticky, add a tiny drop of washing-up liquid to the damp cloth, wipe off and buff dry.

Blinds

Dust settles onto blinds, so next time you have used a tumble dry sheet with your laundry, hang onto that sheet and use this to dust your blinds – the static from the sheet lifts the dust rather than pushes it around

Bedrooms

Bedroom surfaces

A feather duster may seem like a relic of the past, but in a bedroom where we often use dresser tops and bedside tables to store books, eyeglasses, remote controls and so on, that duster will make quick work of your knick-knack-laden surfaces. The nature of gravity being what it is, dust first, vacuum second.

Bed frames

1) Metal bed frames

Dust with a duster or dry microfibre cloth. If you spot any rust spots, brush them away with a stiff wire brush.

2) Wooden bed frames

Shine up your wooden bed frame by applying a wooden furniture polish directly to a cloth and going over the whole structure.

3) Upholstered and fabric bed frames

Grab your vacuum nozzle – or use a lint roller – for a quick refresh.

Mattress

When you are changing your bedding, strip off the sheets and then vacuum your mattress. If you have a turnable one, flip and rotate it so that the head sits now at the foot and the underside becomes the top side. By regularly turning your mattress, you help it wear evenly.

Carpet stains

There are many ways to get rid of carpet stains – from shaving foam, washing-up liquid and laundry detergent, to white vinegar and hydrogen peroxide. Grab what you can as soon as you see the stain, dampen it and then apply the product. Cover with a white tea towel or kitchen towel and leave the product to do the work, approximately 15 minutes. Use this time to have a dust or vacuum around and then come back to your stain. Pat down the towel covering it, then lift away and your stain should be banished.

Iron

After each use, try to get in the habit of giving your iron a wipe with a warm, soapy cloth. If the iron does suddenly stop producing as much steam or has a sticky plate, the quickest method is to wet a magic eraser and then gently wipe over when the iron has cooled, until the marks come off. Alternatively, soak a towel in white vinegar and then, with the iron plate facing down onto the towel, let it sit for 30 minutes, leaving you time to get on and do something else. No scrubbing needed and your iron will be as good as new.

Bathrooms

Toilet brush

Fill a large bucket with hot water, add a few capfuls of bleach and leave the brush to soak. Clean the holder with a disinfectant spray and wipe clean with a paper towel.

Toilet

Scrub your toilet clean by applying a toilet cleaner or bleach, leave it to sit and while the product is working, use a blue microfibre cloth (remember, it is "blue for loo") and wipe the toilet seat and the handle. Then go back to the pan and scrub clean using a hard-bristle toilet brush.

Showerhead

Restore your water pressure by unclogging your showerhead: wrap a towel or cloth soaked in vinegar around the head, leave for 10 minutes and then remove.

Shower screen

A quick way to remove water marks and limescale is to cut a lemon in half, sprinkle with some bicarbonate of soda and rub it all over the screen. Leave to work while you clean out your bath or scrub your toilet. Rinse off.

Tile grout
The key to tile grout is to let the product do the work for you. Apply a mould- and mildew-eliminating product or mix bicarbonate of soda and white vinegar together into a paste and let it penetrate the grout before scrubbing the surface with a stiff-bristled brush. This will make much shorter work of what can be a tedious and exhausting chore.

Laundry basket
We can often forget to clean the laundry basket, but we forget that our dirty clothes can often end up sitting inside the basket for days, creating a nasty odour. Clean by emptying and using a warm, soapy cloth followed by a wipe-down with a damp cloth. Air dry the basket and pop your clothes back in. Keep it smelling fresh by adding a few drops of essential oil to cotton pads and leaving these at the bottom.

Faux-feather duster
Dampen your duster with some warm water and then add a drop of washing-up liquid to the duster. Using your hands, a bit like you are washing your hair, massage the soapy water into the duster, rinse well with warm water and then hang to dry.

Washing machine
For an expeditious washing-machine clean, remove the detergent drawer and soak it in warm water with soap for a few minutes. Spritz the drum with some white wine vinegar, return the detergent drawer dried, and you're done. There's no need to rinse the drum – the vinegar will wash away when you next use your machine.

Tip: Over the summer months, leave the drawer and door open after use for 15 minutes to allow your machine to dry and prevent mould build-up.

Make-up brushes
We use our brushes to apply our make-up regularly. So why is that we never seem to get around to cleaning them? Unwashed brushes can build up bacteria and dirt.

Two of the speediest tips to clean your brushes are:

1)   Swirl a damp brush over a bar of soap, then rinse it in clean water. Keep repeating until your brushes are make-up free.

2)   Mix one teaspoon of coconut oil with a couple of squirts of washing-up liquid and you've got yourself a make-up brush cleanser that deep cleans and disinfects.

How to make your cleaning speedier

One of the best ways to speed up your cleaning is to stop dirt from coming in in the first place. That's why a doormat placed at both the front and back doors of your house is so important.

I always consider my mat to be a bit of a home-security guard for dirt. In my opinion, the best type of mat is a coir mat, as they trap so much dirt.

Speed clean outside your entrance

Get yourself outside and remove anything that doesn't belong in this area. That could be rubbish that has blown over in the wind and ended up trapped in your entrance, or spiderwebs outside the front door (clear these with a broom, and don't overlook the light fittings).

To stop spiders building their webs, wipe the broom head with a little lemon oil before sweeping, and it will transfer onto your outside surfaces as you are cleaning.

Wipe down the door knocker, doorbell and letter box. For any brass, use a specialist brass cleaning product or put a few drops of vinegar onto a microfibre cloth.

Dust the rest of the door with a dry microfibre cloth.

Shake your entrance mat and sweep the path using a good straw broom.

Water any potted plants and remove any dead heads from flowers.

Tip: Occasionally, sprinkle your doormat with bicarbonate of soda and leave for 30 minutes before vacuuming. Feel free to add this into any smelly shoes, too. In either case, the bicarb soaks up any odours.

Speed clean inside your front door

Remove any clutter.

Dust the ceiling and light fittings using a long-handled duster, again with a little lemon oil to stop spiders coming in and building their webs.

Our entrances can take quite a beating with people coming in and out with bags, so it is inevitable that walls in this area will have a few marks. Use a magic eraser to get rid of these, or if that doesn't work, try a very diluted solution of sugar soap applied with a cloth.

Dust any pictures and ornaments, although I don't recommend having too many ornaments in your entrance area, because dust volumes are higher in this part of your home. There is also the danger that items can be knocked over as you are going in and out or by the wind catching them. If you do have these, a blob of Blu Tack on the bottom can help secure them – but only on non-absorbent surfaces, as you don't want to be left with an oily mark.

Wipe down the door handle and the light switch.

Tidy up coats and shoes.

Vacuum and mop the floors.

Water any potted plants and arrange fresh flowers.

Tip: Muddy footprint marks and paw prints can easily be cleaned up with cold water and washing-up liquid.

Tip: Speed up your cleaning by making sure extension cords are long enough before you start to vacuum, there is nothing worse than stopping and starting.

Household tasks you can do in 10 minutes

Do you find that you have pockets of time throughout your day where there isn't time to actually get anything done, but you feel like they're wasted?

It's incredibly frustrating to feel this, but I believe those pockets don't need to be forfeited.

Having a plan for those short windows can make you go from wasting time to being an uber-productive home boss before you know it.

After all, if you can get a lot of the smaller tasks done in these gaps, then you will feel like you have less on your plate overall – and that can only be a good thing, right?

If you can add just one of these things into each day, you may see that your home starts to look more organized, you have more time to do the nicer things in life, you are less stressed when looking around the house thinking of all those things you have to do, and you'll generally be more content with your home – that's a quick win if ever I heard one.

Next time you have 10 minutes free, have a go with one of the tasks on my 10-minute Task Checklist, and then create a list of all those niggling jobs you just don't get around to doing. When you find yourself at a loose end, you can pick something off the list.

10-minute Task Checklist

- [ ] Wrap a present
- [ ] Sort through receipts in your purse or wallet
- [ ] Sort out your handbag
- [ ] Shred a pile of paperwork
- [ ] Sort through magazines and newspapers and take out any interesting articles or recipes
- [ ] Plan a meal
- [ ] Book your online food-shop slot
- [ ] Write an email
- [ ] Check your planner
- [ ] Check your bank balance
- [ ] Book an appointment
- [ ] Open and read your post
- [ ] Put a load of washing on
- [ ] Hang a load of washing out
- [ ] Fold some washing
- [ ] Put away laundry
- [ ] Pre-treat a stain
- [ ] Water house plants and remove any dead leaves
- [ ] Pay an invoice online
- [ ] Meal preparation(e.g. cut up vegetables)
- [ ] Have a quick vacuum around your home
- [ ] Plump up sofa cushions
- [ ] Tidy up the bookcase

- [ ] Dust window seals
- [ ] Dust a room
- [ ] Make the bed
- [ ] Open some windows
- [ ] Put away the dishes
- [ ] Empty the dishwasher
- [ ] Remove dead flowers and clean a vase
- [ ] Wipe down bathroom surfaces
- [ ] Tidy the kitchen
- [ ] Clean a toilet
- [ ] Wipe down the shower screen
- [ ] Tidy up shoes
- [ ] Empty a rubbish bin
- [ ] Replenish toilet rolls
- [ ] Tackle a clutter zone
- [ ] Do a stock check on your dry-food cupboards
- [ ] Quick garden tidy
- [ ] Pull out some weeds
- [ ] Pick up leaves
- [ ] Remove any rubbish from your car

… And don't forget time for you:

- [ ] Read a few pages of your book
- [ ] Take a quick walk
- [ ] Enjoy a cup of tea

Speed up laundry

It is not always easy to keep up with the laundry. There are already 100 other things that you need to do in the day, so adding in another chore that is never-ending can be frustrating and overwhelming.

Follow these tips to help shave time off your household laundry.

One-touch rule

Learning to institute the one-touch rule will help you conquer the laundry pile more quickly than any other tip I have. It is this: when you remove a piece of clothing from a drawer or hanger and you decide not to wear it, return it immediately to the original location. Don't just dump it on your bedroom chair!

If you wear something and think it could be worn again, designate a spot in your closet for that item. Go through the lightly soiled items at the end of the week, double check for stains and determine if they do actually need a wash. One tip is to hang the worn-once garment with the hanger facing backward on your clothes rail, so you know that it has been worn.

Use a garment steamer

A garment steamer is a helpful way to refresh clothes that you have only worn for a short amount of time. If you are one of those people who buys new clothes and then puts them in the wash straight away, this device eliminates the need to do so, as steam both kills bacteria and takes out creases.

New clothes

When shopping for new clothes, always think about how easy the item is to wash and iron.

Shopping wisely is a very important step in making your laundry much easier and will help reduce the number of laundry loads (and the amount of clothes clutter you have). Take time when you are in the shop to read labels and select fabrics that will make laundry easier.

Use more than one laundry basket

Make sure you have a few laundry baskets throughout the home. For practicality, you can place them in bedrooms or bathrooms so that when people undress, they can put their dirty clothes in straight away. In children's rooms, this helps remind them to not leave their clothes on the floor.

By having conveniently placed baskets, you are encouraging other household members to use them, and you won't find a pile of unwashed clothes hidden under the bed or face a backlog of everyone trying to do a mountain of their laundry at the same time.

Have household laundry rules

Enforce laundry rules. Before an item is put into the basket:

* All pockets are emptied

* The item is not inside out

* Zips are all zipped up

* Anything with a stain that needs a pre-treatment is flagged right away

Teach your kids to do the laundry

This is going to be one of your biggest time savers!

Your kids and other family members can do laundry. Teach them how to sort clothes, how to spot treat their stains, how to work the washing machine and dryer and then let them do it. You may need to have them watch you for a while, and then have them do it while you watch them, but after that, let them try it on their own. You can start with baby steps and move on up, but teach them; it's a crucial life skill and a help to the whole household.

Mesh bags

Use mesh bags to stop stray socks from going missing, and bras from getting all tangled up and snagging on other items. Mesh bags are great for these and other delicate items.

Colour code towels and sheets

To make folding and returning clean laundry to the proper spot easier, assign each family member or bedroom a specific colour of towels and sheets. This laundry hack is particularly helpful when beds are different sizes and matching sheets to the right bed is difficult.

Fold clothes straight away from the tumble dryer

Stop moving laundry from basket to basket and then just leaving it to sit there for days so everything gets wrinkled, meaning more work for you. Fold your clothes directly from the dryer, while they are still warm.

Use an over-the-door hanging bar

For items that can't be tumble dried, like long dresses, use an over-the-door hanging bar. Keep this on the back of your laundry-room door so that when you are emptying the washing machine, you can hang up those delicate items straight away.

Have multiple bedding sets

For each bed in our house, I own at least two bedding sets. This makes things easier for when it's time to clean sheets. Remove the old sheets and, after your bed has had a good airing out, add the new. It makes it so you are not in a huge rush to get the dirty ones washed and dried in the same day, but you can also fold them straight from the dryer and put them in the linen closet. This is a sanity saver for kids' middle-of-the-night accidents – you'll already have a fresh set of sheets ready to throw on the bed.

Use towel hooks in your bathroom

Keeping towels off the floor by using hooks means you can use them a few times before having to wash them. Leave your bathroom window open to keep your towels aired out and to speed up drying.

Wash everything properly

Check your clothing tags and follow them; this will save you from most laundry disasters. Make sure you don't use fabric softener on towels, as they will lose their absorbency.

Speed up housework with the power of steam

As I've already mentioned, I love using the power of steam to clean my home. When I get my steamer out, I really do make the most of it.

Cleaning with steam can do wonders for your cleaning routine and save you time. The physical exertion from cleaning is also reduced with steam cleaning, as the steam does the challenging work for you.

If you can, I would highly recommend that you invest in a multipurpose steam cleaner, as these have a range of attachments to tackle various cleaning jobs around your home. A steamer cleans hard surfaces, windows, upholstery and greasy kitchen equipment. The added advantage is you do not have to use any cleaning detergent or solutions, so the power of steam is also kinder to our environment. When steam of a high temperature and pressure, known as dry steam, is applied to surfaces, it lifts dirt, grease and grime with absolute ease.

Water becomes extremely economical when used for steam cleaning: just a single litre of tap water is enough to create 1,700 litres of steam. This is enough for around 20 minutes of high-pressure cleaning.

Removing stubborn grime and grease can be time-consuming with a regular scrubbing brush, but can be dissolved in a matter of seconds with a good steam cleaner. Hard-to-reach areas are much easier to access and clean, and all this without the need for chemicals!

Make sure you never add chemicals to a steam cleaner and only ever use water, as chemicals and essential oils can damage the reservoir.

Some ideas of what you can clean with steam cleaner

Tile grout
Grout is the lines between your tiles that help to stabilize them. They will often become dirtier than the tiles because they're lower and won't be cleaned as efficiently or as often. Grout cleaning can be a tedious job since it often involves bending and scrubbing until your nails are loose. However, steam cleaning grout lines will help to blast away dirt, stains and gunk.

Sealed hard floors
Make sure you avoid using this tool on unsealed wooden or stone floors, as they are porous and prone to damage. The high heat and moisture from a steam cleaner can cause wooden planks to warp.

Refresh fabric sofa and chairs
A steam cleaner is a brilliant tool when you need to clean upholstery, sofas

or fabric dining chairs. Low-moisture steam deep cleans the surface and removes stains without soaking the area and potentially ruining it. Plus, it breaks down odours and kills bacteria. You can also refresh and de-crease curtains.

Grease
Cooking grease on kitchen cabinets and the top of extractor hoods can be annoying and time-consuming to remove – steam clean and that sticky grease will come away easily.

Refresh and remove stains from mattresses
Steam cleaning a mattress is the most effective way to deep clean and sanitize your bed. If you're worried about bed bugs or allergy triggers such as dust mites, a steam cleaner has you covered.

Toilets
Getting down on your hands and knees to deep clean the toilet and toilet area can often be back-breaking; steaming amps up your toilet cleaning and reaches those places that you can't.

Dust your skirting boards
Often overlooked in cleaning, the dust and debris that gather on skirting boards respond to a quick blast with steam.

Disinfect plastic and soft toys
If you have a toddler or baby, you know the importance of keeping toys sanitary. Because babies and toddlers are still developing teeth, they like to chew on everything their tiny hands can grasp.

Rubbish bins both inside and outside
Your bins can easily become a thriving spot for mould, bacteria and odours. In many homes, cleaning the bin can sometimes be left to the last minute. But if you have a steam cleaner, it can be done in no time.

Remove wallpaper
To successfully remove wallpaper with a steam cleaner, you will need to use your steam pad. As the steam penetrates the paper, it will soften the adhesive and you can peel it off easily.

Quickly defrost a freezer
Place a large bowl or container at the bottom of your freezer to catch the ice.
Then simply apply the steam directly into the freezer.

Clean and disinfect pet beds
Most pet beds are far too large to fit in the washing machine, so a steam
cleaner is a great way to clean and disinfect them.

Ten more uses for your steam cleaner
1. Clean car wheels

2. Remove limescale from taps

3. Steam wrinkles out of clothing

4. Clean wired pet cages

5. Dust faux plants and flowers

6. Refresh carpets and rugs

7. De-grease BBQ grills

8. Clean up highchairs and car seats

9. Scrub up shower screens

10. Refresh outdoor furniture

Speedy challenges

Do these three speedy challenges when you feel you want to declutter or get more organized; I'd recommend doing these every other month.

Recycling challenge

Go around your home and collect anything that can be recycled. Recycling could include any of the following items:

* Paper and cardboard

* Plastic

* Glass

* Clothes and bedding that aren't good enough for charity

* Batteries

* Printer cartridges

* Bras
Lots of recycling and waste centres have specific bra banks to donate to, or check out Smalls for All, a charity set up to send bras to those in need in Africa.

* Magazines
Give your old magazines to your local doctor's surgery, dentist or hairdresser and recycle that way!

* Furniture

* Electrical items

The bin bag challenge

Take a black bin bag and try to fill it with anything that is rubbish or needs to be thrown away.

I'll get you started with some ideas of where you will find the rubbish to fill the bin bag.

* Start by emptying all your internal bins from the bathrooms, bedrooms and your lounge – do not include your kitchen bin in this challenge.

* Look through the bathroom and bedroom cupboards for old toiletries and make-up you're no longer using and can't recycle in part or whole.

* Hunt out damaged and broken bits and pieces that can't be fixed, e.g. a glass with a crack in it that really isn't safe to be drinking from, or a kid's toy that is beyond repair.

* Check your dry-food store or pantry for packets and tins that are now out of date.

* Check your fruit bowl for anything that's gone off.

* If you're feeling brave, venture up into your loft – I am sure there is plenty up there to help you complete the challenge.

* Don't forget your shed or garage, either.

Charity bag challenge

Go around your home with your bin bag (or, even better, a canvas tote you can part with) and collect together anything that you no longer need, want or wear, and which someone else may still benefit from.

Once full, take it to your local charity shop or clothes bank.

This challenge tackles those items that you no longer want in your home and that are just adding to your clutter, but which are perfectly good enough for someone else to use.

Charity shops are a perfect way to let these things go and they will be grateful for what you donate. You may want to look for things such as:

* Clothes that no longer fit you

* Clothes that you no longer wear

* Bedding (although only sheets, duvet covers and pillowcases, because most charity shops don't accept duvets and pillows for hygiene reasons, but dog shelters and homeless shelters will welcome these items)

* Towels that are in good condition but no longer match your bathroom colour scheme

* Home accessories, candle holders, picture frames, vases etc.

* Books that you have read and won't read again, or books your children have outgrown

* Pictures

* Costume jewellery and accessories

* Crockery

* Mugs and glasses

* Children's clothes

* Children's toys

* Board games (make sure they have all the pieces)

* Shoes and boots

Unexpected visitors: 10-minute speed clean

Thankfully, these days we have mobile phones, so gone are the days when someone would just literally turn up on your doorstep! It is much more likely that people will call or text before they decide to pop in, so you usually have a good 10 minutes to get your home into some sort of order. Use your 10 minutes of preparation time wisely.

Just focus on the areas your guest will see. If you have clutter from the day built up, grab an empty laundry basket or bucket and clear that clutter, then hide the basket or bucket in a cupboard until they have gone, but do not forget about it. Set an alarm on your phone as a reminder to clear the clutter when your visitors have gone.

* Hide unwashed dishes in the dishwasher. If you do not have a dishwasher, rinse them and stack them neatly by the side of the sink.

* Put any papers, magazines or paperwork you may have out in a neat pile; this seconds-long task instantly makes a room feel much tidier.

* Grab a warm, soapy cloth and quickly wipe down surfaces.

* Throw a clean tablecloth over the table to protect from any possible spillages or crumbs, if you are offering your guests tea and cake.

* Wipe down the entrance door with a damp microfibre cloth with a few drops of your favourite essential oil to give off a fresh smell as they enter.

* Check the toilet is clean. If not give it a really quick scrub with the toilet brush and a little bleach, change the hand towel and spray air freshener.

* Quickly sweep outside the entrance – a tidy entrance always makes a great impression.

Voilà! Your 10-minute speed clean is complete!

Keep it Going

Now that you have created and worked on your ideal cleaning schedule, it is essential that you try to stick with your new routine.

When you develop a new habit, you must remember it is not an instant fix. New habits take time to build into your life: a successful new habit can take between 21 and 66 days to develop.

When you start exercising or go on a diet, you do not see results the very next day. A well-planned exercise plan or diet takes a good few weeks to work, so don't give up if you're feeling the plan you have created is not quite working.

There are a few measures you can take to help you stay motivated and stick with your new routine.

How to stick to your cleaning routine

Don't put pressure on yourself, and start slowly

As with any new activity you do, the first time you try something you will naturally be slower, it takes a while to excel at something.

Your first attempt at a new recipe can be disastrous, but by attempt number 10 you have nailed it, and this is the same for perfecting your home.

If you can't complete all of the tasks you have set yourself in the time frame you have allocated, just stop for the day and continue the next day. As you become better acquainted with your tasks on your schedule, you will gradually make improvements and get faster.

Be adaptable

You created the schedule to fit your needs and typical routine, but any number of things can happen throughout the day to throw your routine off, so try not to get flustered. It is always a good idea to put your phone down or into flight mode so you don't get distracting notifications – a simple text from a friend can throw you right off your plan.

Turn off the TV, as well. Sometimes a good feature on daytime TV is enough to make you switch off and sit down, and before you know it, an hour of your day has gone.

But if you choose not to avoid these distractions, just handle each situation as it comes up. If you couldn't complete your daily cleaning checklist, keep in mind that you can always come back to it later in the day or finish it the following day.

Have your cleaning caddy well stocked and accessible

Instead of wasting time collecting the cleaning products you need for a given task, have your cleaning caddy pre-stocked with all of the products necessary to get any cleaning job done. Create a few caddies and leave one in your bathroom or bedroom, too. Make sure everyone in your household knows where the caddies are and can just grab them to tackle a spill or mess anywhere in your home.

Review your cleaning schedule monthly

Don't be afraid to change your schedule if it isn't working. When we are overwhelmed, it is easy for us to think of ourselves as failures that cannot keep to a simple schedule. But no great person was born great, and each and every one of us must work with what we have and slowly improve with willpower, time and patience. After all, your schedule is not set in stone and there is no such thing as the perfect schedule. If you have overestimated yourself or the time needed to complete all of the tasks, don't just give up. The right fit will eventually come.

Use the wonders of modern technology

Although you may have created the most impressive schedule that certainly deserves a place pinned up in your kitchen, do not underestimate the power of your phone. Use your phone calendar to set yourself daily reminders, so you will be sure not to forget. Sync these reminders with other household members, because housework is about teamwork and not just down to you.

Those phone pings will definitely keep you motivated.

During your cleaning and tidying – which can be boring and monotonous on their own – instead of listening to music, put on an audiobook or podcast to keep you motivated when you are cleaning.

Move with the times

So, with all this in mind, as you start to move through life in your home, your cleaning and organizing needs will change from time to time. You may have just started a family or a new job, so your cleaning schedule will have to change to accommodate that. Then, as your children get older (or if you live with housemates), you can delegate tasks.

By establishing a cleaning routine, and more importantly by sticking to it, you will see that maintaining a clean and tidy home is not as daunting as you once thought. By now, you will probably be enjoying your home so much more, adding in little pops of colour and additional accessories here and there as you go.

Creating a schedule allows you to stay on top of the cleaning and organizing without becoming overwhelmed by the enormity of the tasks, and ensures that you will not be embarrassed to invite people over, or even when unexpected visitors turn up.

You will no longer be worrying about that huge basket of ironing that is hidden in your airing cupboard, or the hallway cupboard that is so cluttered you are scared to open the door. You will have peace of mind and feel much more content in your home.

The benefits of living such an organized life are not just limited to your home, either. By creating and sticking to a good routine, you are able to plan your days ahead of time and give yourself a sense of control over various aspects of your life. When you get invited out for the day by friends, you will be able to switch off and relax knowing that everything is in order.

Family help

Remember housework is not just down to one person — it is all about teamwork. If you are struggling to get the household to pitch in with cleaning tasks, then now is the time to give them a kick up the backside and get them motivated to help you in order to speed up your cleaning and give you all back that precious free time and friends and family time at weekends.

I'm a big believer of everyone helping in the home. Being honest, I do the bulk of the housework, but everyone helps make the house a mess, so everyone should do their part in keeping it clean and organized.

If you've got older kids or teenagers, it's even more important for them to learn to do their own laundry and cook a few basic meals so they know what they're doing when they move out of home. Teaching your children life skills will help them go a long way in life; younger children often love to help out and follow us around when we are cleaning, so try and take advantage of this love of being just like Mum or Dad. It may not last forever!

If we are completely honest with ourselves, we do tend to shower our children with gifts and treats these days, so why not use these gifts and treats as rewards for when they complete their household tasks? Rewards work particularly well with the younger children and you can always make a pretty accomplishments chart too, for their bedroom or the kitchen.

Don't forget to give some variation to the task you give them – doing the same things every day will soon prove to be a big drag. So mix it up, and make sure you give them some days off too.

A good few good tips to instil into everyone that lives in your home are:

* Never ever leave a room empty-handed.

* Always look around the room before you leave it, and if you are going upstairs or downstairs, see if there is an item that you can take so you can put it back where it belongs. You will find that nine times out of 10, there

is something to take with you. This is such a minimal task but can really make a huge difference at the end of your day.

* Tidy as you go.

* Get everyone used to putting their dishes in the dishwasher or sink immediately they've finished, putting their coats and bags away as soon as they get home, and clearing up any rubbish and emptying their bedroom bins when they are full.

Five reasons why you should get the kids involved in housework

New skills   Running a home gives them a huge head start in life and valuable life skills, plus confidence for when they leave home or go off to university.

Respect   If children can see (and get involved) in how much work is involved in running a house, then they will slowly and subconsciously become more aware of what mess they leave around, and how they contribute to the work involved.

It may take some time, but learning what is involved in household chores can really help a child to gain respect for the house.

Teamwork   A family of household members is a team. Teamwork involves listening to others, delegating and working together.

Work ethic   Housework is a great way to get them into that entrepreneurial spirit, which then may lead to proper jobs such as babysitting for neighbours and dog walking.

Self-reliance   Although children should be able to rely on their parents to help them, teaching them the skill of self-reliance as they are growing up is critical for development.

Confidence It builds confidence if they understand how to do things themselves rather than having their hand held the whole time.

Partners

We all want our partners to help out more without having to nag them, don't we?

It's an argument for the ages – who does more around the house? And how on earth do you get your partner to do more?

Couples without a good system for dividing up household tasks get resentful quickly.

So much more can be accomplished by working together than by being upset with one another and feeling unappreciated and overworked.

Here are some basic ideas that, if put into practice, can help you to work together, leading to fewer arguments and less resentment.

1. Nagging
As much as you probably hate nagging, it does work. Well, it does in the short term, because continually pestering your other half to empty the kitchen bin or do a pile of washing-up generally leaves them far too emotionally exhausted to argue back, and they will eventually just do it to shut you up.

2. Remember you are different
Bear in mind that not everyone is the same, and you have probably been brought up differently. The dust building up on the windowsill and the laundry pile getting higher and higher is not necessarily noticeable to them. So, tell them, and ask them to help out and put a laundry load in for you – they may just assume you are happy to do it and take the lead on laundry. Delegation is important.

3. Make a list
Give them a list of chores to do when you are out of the house for the day

and, all being well, by the time you return, the list will have been actioned. A gentle reminder text won't hurt either!

4. Put them in charge
Put them in charge when you are feeling unwell. This will certainly make them feel helpful as well as realize how much you do each day, and hopefully they'll then help out more.

5. Praise them
Sing their praises. They don't need a round of applause or a medal, but a simple and honest thank you after they have tackled a chore can make a big difference.

6. Trade off
Do a trade-off. They may prefer to do the cooking, so let them, and try to align tasks with each person's interests.

Family evening routine

Use your evening wisely, and get the whole family involved in a simple but structured evening routine.

I like to include a few productive tasks and then finish it off with some winding-down tasks, so I'm relaxed enough to sleep.

Your evening routine doesn't need to have a lot of items on the agenda. Having a little bit of cooperative clean-up and preparation for the next day will make your morning much smoother.

Create the 15-minute family power clean-up

Do this at a specific time every evening and put your timer on for it. If you are mainly in the kitchen when the hour approaches, the oven timer is a good one to use and everyone can see it. Get the kids to pick up toys and put items back in their rightful homes. Use a spare laundry basket for this, as they are ideal for holding and moving items around your home.

While the kids are on their mission, now's a good time for the adults to focus on getting ready for the next day.

Here is a typical 15-minute family power clean-up:

* Load and run the dishwasher after your evening meal.

* Wipe down kitchen counters.

* Wipe down the hob.

* Change the tea towel.

* Add the dishcloth to the top shelf of the dishwasher or soak in boiling water overnight, add in a denture tablet to sterilize or a drop of antibacterial cleaning product.

* Have a quick kitchen whizz with the vacuum.

* Have a laundry pile ready to go in as soon as you get up, load and programme your washing machine.

* Take laundry off the washing line or out of the tumble dryer and then fold and put away; don't just leave it piled up on a table or on the sofa.

* Have school and work bags ready.

* Prepare packed lunches and leave in the fridge.

* Have tomorrow's clothes planned out, ready to go.

Your 15-minute family power clean

What will you do in the evening to get your house looking lovely and ready for you to relax before bed?

1...

2...

3...

4...

5...

6...

7...

8...

9...

10...

Household Task Reward Chart

Write each household member's name in the chart below. This doesn't just work for family homes, but in shared houses too. On each day, use a fun sticker to show how many household tasks that person has completed – give each person their own colour or design. Turn it into a contest, rewarding the person at the end of the week who has achieved the most – even if that person is you!

Name	Monday	Tuesday	Wednesday

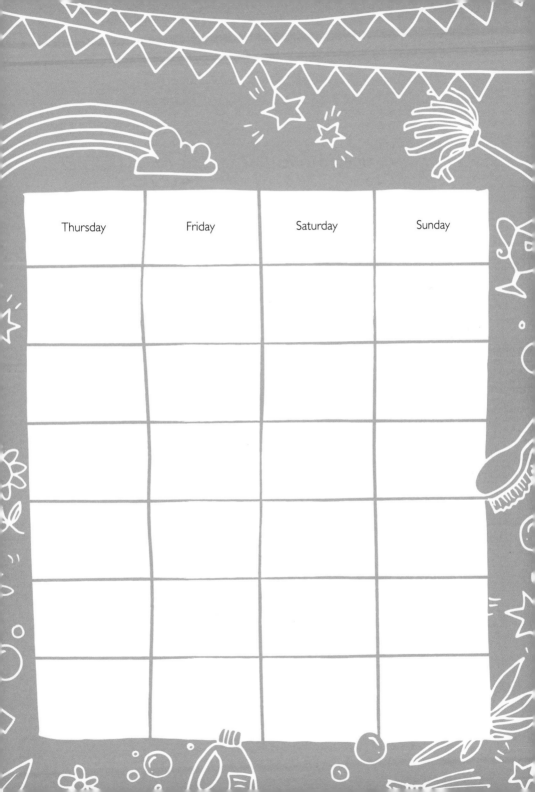

Thursday	Friday	Saturday	Sunday

Getting kids to pitch in

I have put together some age-appropriate tasks that will teach your child valuable skills and make your day that tiny bit easier.

Toddler tasks

— Put their toys away
— Light dusting with a dry duster
— Shake their duvet and plump up the pillows
— Open their curtains or blinds
— Rinse the sink after brushing teeth
— Tidy up loose magazines
— Feed the family pets

Preschool children

Everything toddlers do, plus:
— Make their bed
— Put their dirty clothes in the laundry basket
— Do the washing-up, with safe items such as plastic plates and cutlery
— Set the dinner table
— Put away their ironing if easy to reach
— Replenish toilet rolls in the bathrooms
— Pull up garden weeds
— Sweep the garden path

Older children

All listed so far, plus:
- Help with making the school packed lunch
- Vacuum the floors
- Take out the rubbish
- Collect the mail
- Help sort the laundry into colour piles
- Set and tidy the table after dinner, wipe down table mats
- Pack and organize school bag
- Change over the bathroom towels and mat
- Help to load and unload the dishwasher (safely)
- Help with putting the food shopping away
- Take dog for a walk
- Help make dinner, chopping vegetables (safely)

Teenagers

This is where it starts getting a bit tougher, but they will thank you in the long run. All listed so far, plus:
- Keep room clean and tidy: do a weekly inspection
- Air their bedroom daily
- Wash the family cars
- Cut the lawn
- Clean the bathroom over after they have used it, sink, toilet and bath or shower wipe
- Help with washing the windows
- Strip their beds and put on fresh bedding
- Clean their mobile phones and tablets weekly
- Take the dustbin out on rubbish day
- Organize their own paperwork and emails
- Make dinner once a week and clean up afterwards
- Do some shopping when you are running low on essentials such as bread and milk

Morning routine

Simplify your mornings with a little planning to help you get out the door on time: establish what your "needs", "musts" and "goals" are, and how long your morning routine should last. Your end time should be when you are ready to walk out of the door, to work, to exercise, or to the school run.

Follow the steps below and you'll be heading in the right direction.

Start by ensuring you get enough sleep

If you haven't had enough sleep, you will find it really hard to jump out of bed and function well.

Stick to a sleep routine and go to bed at a reasonable time every night. While you may find it nice to sit on the sofa in the evening and watch TV shows that you aren't really paying attention to or scroll through social channels, you'll feel so much better if you just go to bed.

Once in bed, ditch your phone and read for a few minutes to relax.

A good night's sleep and getting out of bed 10 minutes earlier really will make a difference.

Grab a cuppa

Every morning, I factor in time to have a cup of tea. I sit in a tidy room on my own and catch up on the daily news. I find it really helpful to start my morning feeling relaxed and thinking clearly.

Thinking about your day ahead and taking a deep breath will do wonders for you, but just be careful you don't spend too long sitting down – set a timer if you need to for getting back on track.

Allow yourself extra time in the mornings

Always build in some extra time for this hectic time of day. For example, if you know it takes you exactly eight minutes to drive to your child's school, give yourself 12 minutes. Even when you know something takes a specific amount of time, try to account for surprises.

Be realistic

In this modern, fast-paced world of multitasking, having a jam-packed schedule may seem normal, and even possible, but it's not!

Do not put this immense pressure on yourself. Don't try to cram a load of activities into your short morning routine, or you will end up getting frustrated with yourself.

Focus on getting as much as you can done in your evening routine and leave only the essentials for the morning.

Eliminate those morning distractions

Put down your phone in the mornings to stop yourself from checking your social channels, your emails and your text messages. A flick through the phone in the morning can be such a waste of time – you can get sucked into a WhatsApp conversation so easily, and before you know it, you will be running late, leading to panic and stress.

Leave your phone alone until you have completed your morning routine.

A tip you could try is to pack your phone in your bag. This way, you are less likely to forget it, but because it's out of sight, you're less likely to be distracted by it.

Here's to having a stress-free morning!

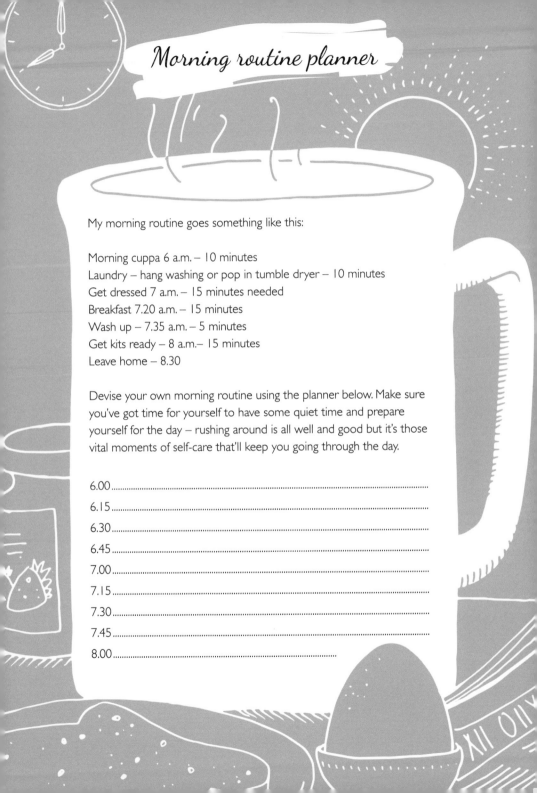

Morning routine planner

My morning routine goes something like this:

Morning cuppa 6 a.m. – 10 minutes
Laundry – hang washing or pop in tumble dryer – 10 minutes
Get dressed 7 a.m. – 15 minutes needed
Breakfast 7.20 a.m. – 15 minutes
Wash up – 7.35 a.m. – 5 minutes
Get kits ready – 8 a.m. – 15 minutes
Leave home – 8.30

Devise your own morning routine using the planner below. Make sure you've got time for yourself to have some quiet time and prepare yourself for the day – rushing around is all well and good but it's those vital moments of self-care that'll keep you going through the day.

6.00 ....
6.15 ....
6.30 ....
6.45 ....
7.00 ....
7.15 ....
7.30 ....
7.45 ....
8.00 ....

Conclusion

Well, I am hoping that by now you are feeling pretty motivated after reading all these ideas and solutions that are going to save you so much time.

Remember, the key here is little and often. Doing a few jobs here and there when you have a few spare minutes will ultimately save you time. Put down your phone when you are boiling the kettle or running a bath and fill these few minutes with something worthwhile. When you bring your laundry in, fold it and put it away straight away rather than leaving the pile to build up. Little changes to your routine and approach to cleaning and tidying will make a huge difference. Instead of treating your cleaning as a huge job to put off until the weekend, it is incorporated into daily life, and you'll barely notice you're doing it – but you will notice how incredibly clean your house is.

Use the checklists I have put together to plan, and refer back to them when you are feeling that you have lost your way a little. Whatever you do, don't beat yourself up if you have gone off track. We all have off days – listen to your body and take a break if you need to. Self-care is so important, and ultimately what we all need in our busy lives.

Remember that cleaning and organizing really doesn't have to be boring. Playing your favourite music and working against the clock will improve your productivity, your mind and your motivation.

An amazing way to keep the motivation going is to use social media to share your cleaning achievements with your followers and set challenges amongst your friends. Use the step chart on page 120 in the cleaning section and record and share your weekly cleaning step count too. I think you will all be really pleasantly surprised at your results!

I would absolutely love for you to share these results with me too. Make sure you mention me, @lynsey_queenofclean, so I can see all of the amazing results from your 15-minute Cleans.

A huge thank you for buying and reading my latest cleaning book, it means so much to me. My love of cleaning came from a very dark place but producing content and writing these books has made me the happiest I have ever been.

Happy cleaning and enjoy your new routine!

Lots of love,

Lynsey QoC

Index

Credits

The publishers would like to thank the following sources for their kind permission to reproduce the pictures in this book.

page 67 Jaoojk3110/Shutterstock, page 85 szefei/Shutterstock, page 91 Savanevich Viktar/Shutterstock, page 186 © Lynsey Crombie

Every effort has been made to acknowledge correctly and contact the source and/or copyright holder of each picture and Welbeck Publishing apologises for any unintentional errors or omissions, which will be corrected in future editions of this book.

Art direction: Amy Honour
Design: Katie Baxendale
Editorial: Isabel Wilkinson
Hair & makeup: Dominika Does
Illustration: Misha Gudibanda
Photography: Michael Wicks

The publisher wishes to thank the following brands for loaning or gifting their products for inclusion in this book:

Addis (www.addis.co.uk)
Dunelm (www.dunelm.com)
Swan (www.swan-brand.co.uk)